NEVER SETTLED

NEVER SETTLED

a memoir of a boy on the road to manhood

SHAWN D. CONGLETON

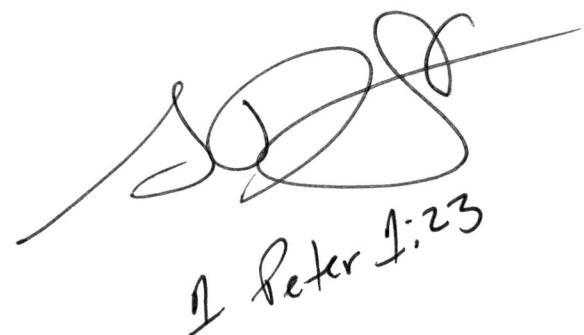

SDC
Shawn D. Congleton

Copyright © 2021 by Shawn D. Congleton

All rights reserved. No part of this book may be reproduced in any manner whatsoever without written permission except in the case of brief quotations embodied in critical articles and reviews.

Unless otherwise indicated, all Scripture quotations are taken from The Living Bible copyright © 1971. Used by permission of Tyndale House Publishers, Carol Stream, Illinois 60188. All rights reserved. Marines' Hymn. Library of Congress, Washington, DC, 2002.
ISBN-13: 9798573878881

Cover design by: Brenna Myers, Lemon's Press
Library of Congress Control Number: 2018675309
Printed in the United States of America

Second Printing, 2021

Contents

PROLOGUE

1	Waking Up (1991)	2
2	Steve (1991)	8
3	Not Moving (1990)	17
4	We Lost Jimmy (1984)	25
5	Loogootee Pt 1 (1980)	34
6	Loogootee Pt 2 (1981)	43
7	Loogootee Pt 2b (1981)	54
8	Dad's beginnings (1947, 1965, 1973 - 1979)	65
9	The Summer Move (1982)	76
10	Loogootee Pt 3 (1982-1983)	88
11	Wandering (1975-1980)	97

12	The Last Days of Jimmy (1983 - 1984)	107
13	From Baby to Leader (1984 - 1985)	116
14	Growing Up Quickly (1985 - 1986)	126
15	Agate, Colorado Pt 1 (1986 - 1987)	137
16	Agate, Colorado Pt 2 (1987 - 1988)	149
17	Northglenn, Colorado (1988 - 1989)	161
18	Byers, Colorado Pt 1 (1989)	168
19	Byers, Colorado Pt 2 (1989)	180
20	Byers, Colorado Pt 3 (1989-1990)	193
21	Senior Year and Beyond (1990-1992)	207
22	Springfield, Ohio (Summer 1992)	216
23	MCRD San Diego (1992)	224
24	Camp Pendleton (1992)	233
25	Forgiveness (1992 - 1994)	241

EPILOGUE
Biographical Timeline 254

1 PETER 1:23 TLB

ACKNOWLEDGEMENTS

About The Author 261

Prologue

What you are about to read may make you want to hate my dad the way I did. Don't. Read the whole story. Don't stop because it gets too hard. I didn't. If it creates too much pain from your own life experiences, take it slow, process it for yourself. Talk to a counselor. Talk to a pastor. Talk to a friend who will help you through it.

My dad, Jim, had some very redeeming qualities. You may see them in the story, you may not. You will certainly read about them in Chapter 25, if nothing else. He also had his own challenges growing up – you will read a bit about those as well. This story is not to belittle my dad. He knows everything he has done. I've told him about it personally.

This is my story about becoming a man. It includes him because he has been a most influential person in my life in so many ways. But I have another Father that was also very influential. You'll read about Him too. Don't stop. *Never settle* for the hard parts. Read it through to the end.

Chapter 1

Waking Up (1991)

I hated that man. I don't understand how some people are allowed to be fathers. My father made my life miserable. He made all of our lives miserable. I never understood how my mother ever put up with him. I was a teenager. Many teenagers hate one or both of their parents. I didn't hate them both. I loved my mom. She was an angel. It took an angel to put up with *him*.

"Get up you lazy piece of sh*t!" my father yelled. I woke out of a deep slumber, startled, wondering if I was about to get pounded. My father had a propensity for violence. I was always afraid of him. He was a big man. I was a little guy. "What the h*ll are you still doing in bed?" he continued to yell. At that point, I was beginning to become more coherent and understand what was happening.

My problem—I was late for school. I worked late the night before and went to bed after midnight. Even after finally getting to bed late, I couldn't sleep since I was still wired from work. Looking at my alarm clock, it was 10:20 a.m. on a school day and here I was still sleeping. That was, until this ferocious grizzly bear came into my room.

"What time is it?" I asked, pretending to be confused. I was still a bit startled, but this wasn't my first rodeo. My only hope was to play dumb. It was my senior year and I had grown accustomed to sleeping in when I felt like it, which was way too often.

"It's after ten and Grandstaff just called me asking why you weren't in school!" he continued to yell. I jumped out of bed and quickly began to gather my things for my shower. My waterbed rocked and rolled as I pressed my way out of it. My room was a mess. Alyssa Milano and other various *Bop* posters papered my walls covering the gorgeous (read as sarcasm) trailer paneling. Clothes were strewn all over the floor. Shoes tossed about. Trash spread over my dresser, end table and the floor. Thankfully, my TV was off. Too often, I fell asleep watching TV. My dad hated that. Wasting electricity and causing my TV to die an early death, he thought.

"I'm sorry. I didn't realize what time it was. I'm headed there right now," I said as I grabbed my clothes and slid out the door of my room. I stealthily slithered between him and the doorway by making myself as small as I could. I moved quickly hoping that he wasn't going to grab me up and beat the crap out of me.

My dad was a large hulk of a man. He had that classic seventies too-long stash and overgrown beard. He wore his wrangler jeans a bit loose, but they were tied up under his large beer belly. He donned the classic country western flannel, half buttoned and loose to stay comfortable. He wasn't wearing any shoes or socks. He never wore socks and his feet were like small stumps. He carried himself like a lumberjack that was twenty years too old and moved with a strong limp due to an injury from a car accident a few years prior. He was almost six feet tall and about 230 pounds. I was only five foot, six inches and 120 pounds. While he wasn't huge by many standards, he may as well as have been *The Incredible Hulk* to me. He was easily as scary, probably more so.

Luckily, I was able to keep moving. I took a quick left, went past the hallway closet with no doors that contained our washer and dryer. Dirty clothes were all over the hallway floor and laying in a pile on top of the dryer. There were clothes stuffed behind the washer and dryer too, but more on that later. *Great*, I thought. *I'm gonna get yelled at for the laundry mess too. That was my brother's job. But, guess who got yelled at any time someone else's chores were not done? Good guess.*

I continued through my brothers' room to the back bathroom that I shared mostly with my mom. I had three younger brothers who were all fairly close in age. They shared the back bedroom which contained a single bed and a set of bunk beds. They each had their own bed, which was rather surprising the more you begin to hear about our lives. Incredibly, we rarely went needing food, clothes or anything else that was truly a necessity. That reality was probably a miracle as much as anything in this story. Their room was a mess too. Toys and clothes everywhere. They were little pigs, kinda like me.

One thing that was rarely in our messy rooms was food. Dad went ballistic if he found food in our rooms. He didn't like our rooms being messy and would yell at us to get them cleaned up, but *HE LOST IT* if there was food or drink left in our rooms. We had lived in enough homes that had bugs and roaches. He knew what attracted them the most; food and drinks left out. That was one of the many things he was a stickler about.

I passed by Shannon's bed (the oldest of my younger brothers) and quickly slipped into the back bathroom. I closed the door, hoping that he wasn't following me back to the bathroom and that I had escaped his wrath. Silence. For a moment. But it was quickly followed by loud music coming from the front of our trailer. *"Dixieland Delight"* by Alabama had begun blaring on the stereo.

My dad had meandered his way past the pool table in our "dining room", past the large dresser blocking the opening to the living room and past the record shelves back to his spot that held his desk. Tears streamed down my face. That was close. I thought I was a goner. I may have deserved to get yelled at for sleeping in and not going to school, but I thought, for a second, he would finish me.

I never knew how serious my dad would take the biggest or the smallest thing. Today, he might be assessed for a mental imbalance or emotional disturbance — I just thought of it as characteristic of his alcoholism. He could be a mean, angry old man that could turn on me in a second.

I quickly showered and headed off to school, not stopping to let my dad know that I left. I passed the pool table in our "dining room" and went out the back door of our trailer, which was positioned next to the kitchen. As I exited the trailer, I jumped over the fence that was near and got into my first car —— a 1976 Chevy Ventura. I bought it from my parents with my own money that I had earned working. I made payments of fifty dollars over five months. Outside of that, allowing me to buy the car, they didn't really do me many favors. They bought it for two hundred fifty dollars and then sold it to me for the same price, but on payments, just like our seven rent-to-own VCRs & four TVs.

At first, I loved that car! I mean, it was my first and I did buy it with my own money. It was grayish silver and had a black racing stripe down the middle. I always thought the front of the car looked like a mix between a Camaro and a Mustang while the back looked like a Nova. It was like if you were from the seventies and went to Woodstock and lived like you were in the movie *"Dazed and Confused,"* at the same time. It was *that* cool! Until you put it in drive.

I turned the key and the car roared! It screamed like no other. It had a glasspack muffler and it roared to life. You might have thought you were at a drag race when I revved the engine. I put it in reverse, pulled out of my parking spot and onto the roadway in front of our trailer. I came to a stop, put it in drive and hit the gas. The engine raised, my pulse quickened and the car blared. Then it whimpered and puttered at about twenty miles an hour down the dirt road from our trailer. Yes, it whimpered and puttered.

This car had no power. It just sounded and looked cool. You could floor it and it still only moved at a snail's pace. I was so embarrassed. It sucked because as a young man, it looked and sounded the part, but had nothing in terms of performance. However, it did provide one very important thing for me. I was free. I left our trailer and that horrifying man behind. I was free of fear for a period of time. Until I had to go home again, which I tried to do as little as possible.

I worked at *The Golden Spike Inn*. This was our local, small town steakhouse in Byers, Colorado. I started as a dishwasher at fifteen years of age and progressed into becoming an assistant cook throughout the rest of high school. I wanted a job so bad since we were poor and my parents never had money to buy me what I wanted. We got what we needed, but we rarely got what we wanted. So, I went looking for a job like my dad admonished.

Mom was the family breadwinner at this time in our lives so all of us kids had chores at home. My dad was a fairly typical man of the seventies and believed housework was primarily for women and children. Since Mom worked long hours and drove an hour to and from work, us kids were assigned all of the housework. The oldest kid at home generally cooked dinner, washed the dishes and cleaned the kitchen. The other kids did the laundry, restrooms, trash, and the rest of the house cleaning. However, once I got a job, dad surprisingly allowed me to only maintain my own bedroom. I couldn't even do that right. I mean, I was a teenager.

I was a mix of responsible and irresponsible at the same time. Like many teenagers, I was responsible for what I wanted to be responsible for and that was about it. I was also very irresponsible for things that I didn't care much about. In that sense, my story begins much the same as any teenager, however there wasn't much about my life that was normal. Normal was something I had always wished for, in our family. Sometimes, I found it for brief moments in the lives of my friends. That's what Steve gave me; a bit of normalcy.

Chapter 2

Steve (1991)

As I drove to school from our trailer about a mile out of town, I drove right past *The Golden Spike Inn* that I had left about 11 p.m. the night before. Just before I got to school, I stopped by my friend Steve's house. He lived about a block from the school and his house was like my second home. He tended to skip school a lot and I knew that his mom was at work about an hour away. Steve's dad lived in Ohio and his younger sister was always at school when she was supposed to be, so we sometimes hung out at his house instead of going to school. We never really did anything too bad like smoking dope or drinking. We just hung out. We both thought drinking and using drugs were stupid, so we made good friends.

I pulled into his driveway, but could not tell if he was home because Steve didn't have a car. He had to walk everywhere he went or bum a ride from me, which was most of the time. I decided to go ahead and check. I walked up the driveway to his bedroom window on the right side of the house. I peered in his window, didn't see anything, so I tapped lightly on the window. No response. I walked back around to the front door and lightly rapped on it as if I was hiding my presence and announcing it at the same time.

Steve peered out through the small diamond window in the door. We both smiled.

"Brutha!" he said in a high pitch voice as he opened the door. We exchanged a guy hug and I entered his home. He was watching tennis and eating a large bowl of *Fruity Pebbles*. When I say large bowl, what I really mean is a large mixing bowl! And he ate with a large mixing spoon! That was his favorite. Steve was always pretty generous and would let you eat his food and hang at his house, but he didn't share his *Fruity Pebbles*. Those were his.

"What are you up to?" I asked as he waved me in.

"Watching Jennifer Capriati! Can you believe she is only fourteen?" he exclaimed. Steve was a bit infatuated with her and for good reason. She was a good looking girl, but she was even more impressive as a tennis player. She was in the top twenty-five female players at the age of thirteen years old and was competing at the highest level tennis tournaments at fourteen years of age. Here we were, sixteen and seventeen years old ditching school, hanging out and eating bowls of cereal in small town Colorado.

We both had dreams and visions of escaping this place. We knew we were meant for more. We just had no idea what it was yet. That was another thing we had in common. Steve and I didn't fit in this small town. We had suburban-style dreams, but were stuck in this western country-style, podunk community like Kevin Bacon in *Footloose*.

We dressed in our urban hip hop getup, wearing our all blue *Adidas*, *Skidz* pants, *Z. Cavariccis*, and Bart Simpson's "Don't have a cow man!" t-shirts. Everyone else in this little town dressed in *Wranglers* or *Lee* jeans and cowboy boots. We were so out of place. While many of our peers in Byers listened to country western music and classic rock, we listened to the popular R&B tunes of the day such as Boyz II Men, Janet Jackson, All-4-One, and the like.

Steve was always so positive and fun! He was the life of the party and he had this confidence about him that made me feel better about life. He was THE fun guy! Although he was a year younger than me, he always taught me things like how to dance, how to talk to girls and whatever the latest style was. He was also much more athletic than I was, five or six inches taller and forty pounds heavier. So he excelled as our starting tailback while I was relegated to fourth-string fullback. I did excell in wrestling though, as a state qualifier for two years while Steve struggled to crack the lineup in basketball. Yet, we were great friends and hung out all the time! We loved a lot of the same things and he helped me enjoy life more when otherwise, I may have just been depressed about my lot in life.

"Are you going to school today? My dad just woke me up because Grandstaff called him asking where I was," I explained to him.

"Probably not. What's the point? The French Open is only on this week. Besides we can have more fun here!" Like Ferris, Steve was too focused on having fun versus some of the other important aspects of life. Don't get me wrong. He did want to be successful with his life, but if he didn't see the point, he didn't give it too much attention.

"I don't know. I just wonder how much trouble we will get into. I'm sure they will figure out we are hanging out together." I expressed my concern, but the fact that I was there at all was proof about how much I cared. "I've got all A's for the most part anyway. I'm so glad that I am almost out of this school and town!"

"Let me finish my cereal. Looks like Capriati is going to lose this match. It's incredible what she's done to this point as it is!" Steve explained. We hung out another half hour. Steve finished his cereal and Capriati lost.

We got in my car and drove up to the school. We tried to park in the back and *sneak* into school wearing shorts (which weren't allowed). We were such goofs, always trying to get away with stuff we felt like doing. We came in through the back doors, and snuck in through the locker rooms and the commons area. Anyone we passed by, we just pretended we had been there all along as if we belonged where we were, and that we were wearing pants. Usually, they just went along with it.

It's interesting to think about now. I acted like I didn't really want to be there and I took advantage of opportunities to miss school, but really, I loved that place. I always had. School was usually a very positive place for me where teachers and adults actually cared, even when I didn't. When I was at home, I never knew when my dad was going to blow up. I was always on pins and needles. What chore did I forget to do? What did I mess up now? What did one of my brothers do that I was going to get in trouble for? It was easier to be at school, less responsibility and even fewer negative consequences. If I got in trouble at school, the most they typically did was shake their head in bewilderment. Thankfully, I rarely got in trouble at home for my school discipline. As long as I was passing my classes and did not get in trouble with the law (which wasn't always the case), I was fine at home. I didn't know what was going to happen that morning that I was late to school, but honestly my dad never mentioned it again. He was just angry in the moment.

Fourth period was just getting started and it was time for me to finally find class. I walked into my Vocational Business class, which was actually third AND fourth period. I missed third obviously, so Mrs. Adamson asked, "Where have you been? You missed all of third period." She was calm. She liked me and treated me well.

"I just got to school. I woke up late. Sorry," I explained.

"No problem. Did you finish chapter three? You have to type the entire first section," she replied.

"Yeah, I finished chapter three the other day. You want me to teach this class for you?" I joked.

I typically helped her out a lot that year because we got new computers at the school. I never received formal computer training, but I could just sit down, start playing with it and figure it out. I did a lot of that for her that year. She didn't understand the operating system and how everything worked so I played with it and showed her. I was one of the most prolific male typers since I had taken typing my freshman and sophomore years. Back in that day, for some reason guys weren't that great at typing. The females were typically much more prolific. I prided myself on being able to keep up with the girls and quite often, even surpassed them.

It was amazing that I could even do anything positive at school. We *never settled* in one town very long. We moved many times a year, almost every year. Due to the number of times we moved, my education was constantly disrupted. I also had a propensity to have behavioral issues from time to time at school. I excelled academically everywhere we went and most often surpassed those that had been at that school all along.

I enjoyed the positive reinforcement I received at school from my teachers. Positive reinforcement was severely lacking at home and it was nice to receive it from somewhere. It motivated me to do well in the classroom. I *never settled* for just passing my classes either, but pursued excellence knowing that I would receive more positive feedback from my teachers.

"Hey, can I go to the library to work on a project for English?" I asked.

"Since you finished typing the first section, sure. What do you have going on?" she asked.

"I am working on my Senior English paper. I'm almost finished, but need a few more resources. I'm writing about 'Bart Power,'" I explained.

"Bart Power? What's that?"

"Bart Simpson. He gives me power. I wear his t-shirts almost every day. I watch his show every week. The cheerleaders gave me a Bart doll and made him a Byers singlet and headgear. Every match I wrestled this year, he sat matside and gave me power. I didn't go to State on my own, you know?!" I laughed. She shook her head in bewilderment and then wrote me a pass.

However, I did not go to the library although I did indeed need to finish that paper. That was all true, but I also knew fourth period gym class was playing basketball and I loved playing basketball. I wasn't very good since my body was better built for wrestling, but I loved to play.

I went into the gym and saw Steve and my other buddy, Kent, playing. I jumped in the game and played most of the period. Nobody in our small school questioned any of it. That's how we got away with so much. Unfortunately, after playing for about thirty minutes, I ended up spraining my ankle pretty badly. Kent escorted me down to the nurse's office where I received ice, a wrap and some crutches for the rest of the day.

"Man, you were actually playing pretty decent today before you got hurt!" Kent said.

He was always very encouraging to me. He would always say uplifting stuff like he was trying to build my self-esteem. I don't think he did it intentionally, I think he just felt so bad about himself and his own life that he was always impressed with someone else and what they were doing. Nevertheless, I appreciated it and that was one of the reasons we were such good friends. Kent also lived in the same trailer court as I did. Like Steve, he bummed rides off of me since he didn't have a job or a car. He only had a couple of friends and I appreciated him befriending me when I first moved into town two years prior. I hobbled back to my Vocational Business class on the crutches.

"What happened? Are you okay?!?" my startled teacher asked when I arrived.

"Yeah, I'm okay. I just sprained my ankle playing basketball with the gym class," I explained. My teacher just shook her head. She knew she gave me a pass to the library and that I did not go where I was supposed to go. She didn't say another word about it though, probably figuring my injury was enough punishment.

Later that day, in sixth period English, I was brought back to my school reality. We were working independently, but our teacher was out and the sub was just kind of hanging out, it seemed. I say that because several kids in that class didn't care much for me and loved to pick on me there.

As I mentioned earlier, I wasn't a very big guy. Never was. I was always small for my age and a bit of an introvert if I didn't know you well. This led me to getting picked on a lot at school over the years, particularly due to always being the new kid. While I wasn't new here anymore, these kids were starters on the football team and thought they ran the school. I'm sure I said something smart to them because I did run my mouth from time to time. That kind of went hand in hand with being small –– little guy, big mouth.

Those guys weren't having any of it. They started making jokes about me, probably about my size or something that didn't even make sense. You would think a two-time state qualifying wrestler wouldn't have to deal with that stuff. But, I did. Since I was always small for my age and perennially the new kid, I blamed my dad for it. If we hadn't moved all of the time, I would have developed better long-term friendships and acceptance at school, I told myself. I would have known how to respond better to those kinds of situations. I would not have always felt like the outsider. But, we **never settled** and this was my life.

"Dingleberry!" this kid called me.

"What? What the heck is that?" I asked, trying to ignore him and brush it off.

"You're a dingleberry!" The class lost it. They all started laughing and were just dying. I had been called many names throughout my school career. The most prominent at this school was Congledong. I never lived that one down. But, this kid was calling me *Dingleberry*. It made no sense. No one even knew what it meant. This ignorant kid didn't even know what it meant. He just blurted out some word that sounded funny and off putting. It was. On both accounts.

I got up to go after him, but he caught me coming. He shoved me aside and I went flailing to the ground. My ankle had almost recovered from the morning, but now I reinjured it. The whole class started laughing again.

"You better watch yourself, *Dingleberry*. You're gonna get yourself hurt!" he sneered. The sub finally jumped in and broke it up. He sent me to the principal. Me. He sent *ME* to the principal. That was about par for the course. I was always the one getting in trouble for stuff that other people did to me.

I sat in the principal's office that day and listened to my dad on the other end of the phone. My mind raced and I wondered what was going to happen. Would he be on my side? Would he be furious at me? Would I get beat when I got home? What would my punishment be? I was sweating it and angry at the same time. How was I the one in the principal's office to begin with?! But, I heard my dad on the other end of the line yelling at the principal.

That was my dad. He didn't care who it was. He let them have it. He seemed to like being angry and yelling. He did it a lot. After Dad finished yelling at the principal, the principal released me to go home with a one-day in school suspension to be served the next day. I couldn't believe it. I was in trouble for what someone else did to me. *The story of my life*, I thought. The school day was almost over, so I headed over to Steve's and waited for him to come home from school.

After Steve came home, we hung out for a while and talked about sports. Eventually, though, we also talked about the fact that we wanted our lives to really mean something. We weren't going to be stuck in this small town with no future the way we saw many of these farm boys. We **never settled** for that way of life. Steve had a way of giving me vision for my own life. He had a way of encouraging me and making me feel better about myself.

Later when I got home, my dad yelled at me for a bit, but he hated school officials way more than me. I didn't really get into too much trouble since he figured it was just as much their fault as it was mine.

My biggest problem was that my dad always wanted to move. He **never settled** in one place for very long. As soon as I started to enjoy something about a particular place we lived, we had to leave it. Like the year before, in Byers, when my dad tried to move us after living there for only a year.

Chapter 3

Not Moving (1990)

"You really think your mom will let me live in the garage?" I asked Steve.

"Sure! We'll talk her into it. She loves you Cong! She'll let you do anything. She lets *you* drive our car and she won't even let *me*! Once we tell her why, she'll definitely let you," Steve explained.

"I would love to fix this place up. We could move all of this storage and junk over to the side and then put a bed in there and fix up that old stereo. This will be so sweet! Like my own apartment!"

"Let's do it now! We'll surprise her!" Steve encouraged.

My dad was talking about moving again. I was done. I hadn't told him yet; but if they moved, I was staying. We had lived in Byers for just over a year. This was the longest I had ever gone to one school. A year was our longest stay in one house my entire life. I'm not really sure why he wanted to move again, but he said we were. Now that I was in high school, I didn't want to move. In elementary, and even junior high, it wasn't really that big of a deal. Looking back, I liked the changes and the prospect of something always being better than where we were.

Now, in high school, I was much more into wrestling and girls. There was no way I wanted to move again. We had a great wrestling team at Byers! I qualified for the state tournament, which was an incredible accomplishment for me.

I first learned how to wrestle in the sixth grade. We had only lived in Hudson for a few months, but during that time, my friend Tony talked me into wrestling. He had wrestled for several years and was quite good. He won most of his matches. Me, on the other hand, I lost most of my matches. Okay, honestly, I lost all of my matches that first year. My only wins were by forfeits, when the other guy didn't show or had been injured. But, I had developed a strong base and good foundation for the sport. My favorite part of wrestling was, I actually got to compete against other kids my size.

I was always a small kid, tiny really. During that sixth grade year, I wrestled in the sixty-four pound weight class. My own daughters, all pretty small and skinny for their age were all bigger than I was at that age, but I loved sports and competing! Problem was, I was too small to be very competitive at most of them. Second problem, I was also slow. In athletics, typically the little guys are quick. That's their advantage. But, not me. I was both small and slow. And not the most coordinated either. But, as I participated, I developed more coordination as I practiced each sport. While I never gained much speed to the point of being considered *fast*, I did develop some quickness. This helped me develop into an excellent wrestler in high school.

The problem was, after we moved from Hudson in the sixth grade, I didn't attend another school that offered wrestling until the tenth grade. That year, we moved into the suburbs, which was something we never did. We always lived in small towns or sometimes in the country. That helped us keep a low profile.

Keeping a low profile was important to my dad. It helped him stay off the law enforcement radar. After all, he had quite a few DUIs over the years and a few bouts with my siblings and I being taken and placed into foster homes for periods of time. So, we did our best to lay low and stay off their radar by taking the-road-less-traveled.

My sophomore year, we lived in the suburbs: Northglenn, Colorado. For the first time, I attended a large, suburban high school. Their wrestling program was huge! They had a solid basketball program, as well. For a while I was hoping to do both because I loved basketball too! I played basketball at many of the schools between my sixth grade year and my sophomore year and really enjoyed it. But, I was too tiny. And slow.

In the ninth grade, I attended the smallest of schools: Agate, Colorado. Agate was a small town, public high school in Colorado. The town itself was four square blocks. There were only eighteen total students in grades nine through twelve. The class size my freshman year had almost doubled from the previous year. We grew from three students in the eighth grade to five the following year. There were eight guys on the high school basketball team. There were only nine in the entire high school. Speaking of being tiny and slow, I was right about five feet tall as a freshman and less than a hundred pounds. I didn't play much, but I did enjoy the game.

Now, as a sophomore at this large, suburban high school, I was competing to play basketball in their summer league and also wanted to wrestle since I was finally at a school that offered it. I started to love basketball because I loved watching the Chicago Bulls and Michael Jordan play in his early years. He was such an incredible player to watch. People argued about who the best basketball player was at that time; Magic Johnson or Larry Bird?

I argued it was Michael Jordan ever since his rookie year in the league. It seemed that Michael could score at will. Whenever he was driving to the basket, he would stick his tongue out with swagger, knowing he couldn't be stopped. I remember learning that summer as I was trying to make the basketball team that Michael Jordan didn't even make varsity his sophomore year in high school. I figured I would be a late bloomer, as well, just like Michael Jordan.

After practice one day, I found out that I would not be able to play basketball and wrestle during that next school year. Even though I loved both sports, I would have to choose. Many would say I chose wisely. My tiny body was fit for wrestling, not basketball. By this point, I had grown in height and weight, but I was lucky if I was five feet, three inches and only around one hundred and ten pounds – so I chose wrestling.

Our wrestling team at Northglenn had about fifty wrestlers, which included about four or five guys in each weight class. We had a very competitive room during practice. The coaches were great, but since I had only wrestled one year, I didn't have a lot of experience.

Experience in high school style wrestling is everything. Take a guy with a couple of years wrestling experience and he will beat a guy fifty to a hundred pounds larger than him with no experience every time. The great part about wrestling for me was that I was able to compete against other guys my size once my experience caught up.

Wrestling is broken down into twelve or thirteen weight classes. I wrestled in the one hundred and twelve pound weight class that year; a highly competitive weight class at Northglenn. I held my own against most of them, since I did have that one year of experience, but I hadn't improved enough to wrestle varsity. I was able to wrestle junior varsity that year and actually had a winning record with fourteen wins and thirteen losses. I was stoked! I found my sport and tasted some success!

While fourteen wins and thirteen losses doesn't seem like much success, it was for me. My athletic endeavors prior to that were very limited. I had played basketball in the eighth grade in tiny Agate. Since that school was so small (remember three eighth graders), we played **co-ed** basketball. That means, girls played too. In fact, two girls started over me on the basketball team. A little embarrassing to a guy, but hey, those girls were pretty good! I did come off the bench and played a little bit, though. I enjoyed it, but seriously *TWO girls started over me*. One of them was in the grade below me.

In the traditional girls sports at this small school, we were in the same situation with co-ed participation. Guys were allowed to play girl sports, such as volleyball so I played on the eighth grade girl's volleyball team. Luckily, I was a starter in volleyball though. I played pretty well and loved it, but my size still left a bit to be desired.

In the ninth grade, at that same school, we had six-man flag football. I really enjoyed it too. You would think with flag-football that my size wouldn't be as big of a deal. It wasn't. But, my speed was. I was too slow. It's hard to explain to a non-athlete just how slow I was, but just accept that I was the slowest guy on the field and it wasn't close. I rarely played even six-man flag football with only eight guys on the team. I loved playing sports, but never had much success.

That was why wrestling JV my sophomore year at a large suburban high school and winning fourteen matches while only losing thirteen was a huge accomplishment for me. I knew I had found my sport.

Here we were at the end of my junior year now, living back in the small town of Byers. I had found even greater success by winning twenty-three matches and only losing ten my junior year, including wrestling in the state tournament. I remember meeting up with that sixth grade wrestling buddy at State,

Tony. He placed fourth that year. I was just excited to be there and was glad to have improved so much.

I was incredibly proud of my success as a state wrestler. Since my home life was so miserable and my parents didn't support my wrestling or academic endeavors, I was proud of that accomplishment. I also knew that most of my accomplishments came from hard work and self-determination. I *never settled* for just being good at wrestling, I worked hard to be the best and I stuck with it.

Now, after my junior year of wrestling, Dad was trying to take that away. I just knew he was going to move somewhere that didn't have wrestling again. Or that he wouldn't even know or care before he chose the next place. After all, he hadn't bought any of my wrestling gear. He hadn't paid for my wrestling camp. He didn't even attend a single one of my wrestling matches, until the state tournament that year.

On a whim, he decided to drive my mom to work since there was a snow storm and as he was driving her home, they stopped back at McNichols Arena in Denver to watch my match. That was the only match he ever attended.

My dad had a way about him that was so selfish and focused on what he wanted. He told me that he never came to any of my matches because he disliked the sport. He tried it in high school, but didn't do well and didn't care for the sport. However, he loved football and basketball, but never came to any of my games in those sports either. I thought, if you loved your kid, you offered your support by showing up. That's how I saw it. He didn't.

Here we were, the day after my dad got drunk and was about to throw a pool ball at me (more on that later) and he was threatening to move again. I wasn't going back home. I was done. I had to convince Steve's mom to let me move in with them. I had to come back for my senior year to compete and place at State. I wasn't going to let him take that away from me.

"Whattya say, ma?!! Can I move in??? I won't bother you. In fact, Steve and I have already figured out how we can rearrange the garage so that you won't even hardly see me," I pleaded with Cathy, Steve's mom. I always called her "ma" when I wanted something. She loved that sort of thing. I thought that if she felt a familial obligation, she would be more likely to help me. I hoped.

"I don't know Cong," she told me. "You can stay for a few days while you guys sort this out, but you can't live in my garage for a year!" She explained.

I didn't mind living in the garage! It seemed like a great idea. A far better idea than dealing with my dad and definitely better than moving again. I had to figure something out because I was done living this nomadic lifestyle. I needed something more, something better. I needed some hope in my life. I wanted something better. I wanted my life to BE better. I was tired of all the moving and I needed some stability to launch myself into the next part of my life. I also needed a great senior year of wrestling to move forward to whatever was next, maybe even wrestling in college. I was done with the moving life. I would *never settle* for that life.

Moving had not *always* been a bad thing. In many ways, it was all I had ever known. When I was a younger kid, it didn't matter as much. Until around sixth grade, I had been a passive observer of my life. I didn't know how life was supposed to be, how it could be. But, when I became a teenager, I began to make choices and do things that I cared about. I began to *live* the life I wanted, even if it was in small bits.

Now that I was older, sports mattered. Friends mattered. Wrestling mattered. I couldn't go back to that life that we had always known. I was ready to leave home in high school like my older brother, Jimmy. Like my older sister, Terri. I thought I was destined to be the first kid in our family to graduate while still living with our parents, but now I wanted out. I just didn't know if I could do what Jimmy did.

Chapter 4

We Lost Jimmy (1984)

When I say I moved a lot, it's not in the way one might think. After I tell people this, their next questions are usually, "Was your father in the military? Was he in the ministry?" Families who "move a lot" due to ministry or military don't compare to my experience. Those that have served in the military, their families typically move every one to three years at most. For those that have served in the ministry, the average pastoral stay is about three and a half years. Actually, my family stopped moving when I entered high school. I only went to four schools during my high school career. That was an average of once per year. After we stopped moving.

For many years we moved every couple of months. Sometimes more. I remember coming home from school having no idea that we were moving again and the car would be half-packed. It was our goal to finish packing and get out of town before the sun went down. As a child, this way of living was really not a big deal. It was all I knew. I never developed a friendship long enough for it to impact me too much when I left. I didn't attach to anyone long enough to have issues with detachment. My life was lived on and off the road.

We didn't move with pick-up trucks or U-Haul rentals either. We moved with one car, loading as much as we could carry in one trip. Did I mention, I have six siblings? Only five of us kids lived at home at one time though, since the older ones were out of the house before the younger ones were born. My older brother and sister each ran away just before or during their freshman year of high school. They were four and six years older than me, respectively.

"Where's Jimmy?" I asked as we were loading the car.

"He'll be here or we'll pick him up," mother assured me.

We had been loading the car for a few hours and were getting close to being done. Our trailer home was mostly cleaned out of our belongings. There was trash strewn throughout and it certainly wasn't empty, but most of the belongings that mattered to us were now out. As was common though, as soon as I thought we were almost done, I would find many more things yet to finish. Below the sink in the kitchen, the bathroom, and the lesser used closets hid many of the commonly needed items that needed to go with us.

"Get all of the bath towels and the extra blankets out of the closet!" Dad yelled. He was tying the load on top of the car.

Our car was a 1973 Chevy Impala. We had a typical way of packing that was pretty efficient; all things considered. This required one of these classic large box cars from the sixties or seventies! On top of the roof of the car would be a mattress and a set of box springs. This would provide a platform for the first row of boxes. We would stack one, two, or three rows of boxes on top of those. Then we would add another mattress, the box springs on top, and tie the load up. Ties would go around the sides and through the windows and also around the front of the car. If we had a kitchen table, it would be placed upside down on top. The kitchen chairs were placed over the table legs to secure them. Other kinds of loose furniture items would follow suit such as end tables, headboards, and even our bicycles would be strung over the table legs.

The back seat was removed and placed on top of the open trunk. The back seat area was filled with household goodies until it reached level with the top of the front seat. Then blankets were put down so that the kids could ride in the back, laying on top of those household goods covered by the blankets as we traveled. In the front seat was a hard ice cooler that one of us rode on top of and used as a seat. Dad and Mom sat in the front with one kid and the rest would lay down in the back and even in the back window ledge. That was a place of glory where the sun would shine through. It held an incredibly warm view and the beautiful sunshine put me right to sleep.

The trunk was opened up so that it could be filled with all sorts of goodies. The trunks of many vehicles were huge in that time and we filled the trunk up beyond its ability to close. The trunk lid sat at a 45 degree angle facing the sky, packed full with the back seat on top of it. That would all be tied down of course with some good *Ace Hardware* rope. It was a pretty tight concoction. One I've never seen anywhere else. Those that did see it, usually gawked until we left their sight.

Our overloaded car was like Joad's truck pulling out of the driveway headed to our next stop in life. My bike and my sister's tricycle were both on top of the car, layed over the upside down table. My older brother, Jimmy's bike was not. I went looking for it around the backside of the trailer where we parked our bikes. *Where was his bike?!?* I wondered. My brother and I loved to ride bikes. We rode them all over town. They gave us a sense of freedom. We could go wherever we wanted, whenever we wanted. I suppose that was the same sort of freedom my dad was looking for by moving every few months.

The previous summer, when my brother Jimmy was thirteen and I was nine, the two of us rode our bikes nearly twenty miles from Seymour to Columbus, Indiana one Saturday. We had one mission that day—-buy Dad twenty dollars worth of blank audio tapes.

My dad used his audio tapes to record mix tapes of his record albums. He had a few purposes for recording mix tapes. First, he wanted to make sure all of his albums played scratch free. He had to ensure that his albums were in superb playing condition. Second, he would play these tapes when friends were over shooting pool at our house. He always provided the background entertainment with these tapes and they were definitely a topic of discussion. My dad poured out his knowledge of music, the artists and where they charted, for how many weeks, and in what year. Lastly, he also sometimes recorded mixtapes to give to people. My dad liked to bless people with music! He loved music so much and it gave him great joy to share his music with others. He would often give one of his mixtapes away; sometimes for money, sometimes in trade, and sometimes as a peace offering with a stranger.

Our mission that day was to pick up twenty dollars worth of audio tapes from the store that had a sale. Our assets were forty dollars in food stamps. Dad gave us forty dollars in food stamps to accomplish our mission. One might wonder, "Huh? I thought food stamps could only be used to purchase food?" Yep, they are right. But, this was the 80's and we perfected the way to use food stamps to get whatever we wanted.

In that time, when we purchased a food item with a food stamp, the store gave us back normal coins as change. Therefore, we went into a store, bought a cheap food item for as low cost as possible and retrieved as much coin change as possible. The best items for us, as kids, were things like cheap candy bars. If we found a twenty cent candy bar, we got eighty cents return on the dollar and had a tasty treat at the same time! However, we had to do this multiple times at multiple stores at multiple registers to keep from raising suspicion. Our goal was to end up with at least twenty dollars in coin change. The problem was that we could only eat so many candy bars in one day.

My next best option I found was an onion. I could buy a single onion for about ten or fifteen cents. When I bought an onion, that helped too because it also prevented suspicion. No one questioned the legitimacy of a kid using a dollar in food stamps to buy an onion. Plus, my return was even greater at about eighty five to ninety cents on the dollar! Of course, we just tossed the onion away and moved on to the next foolhearty cashier or store. Dad said we could keep or use whatever money was left.

We rode our bikes to that next town that Saturday, spent the day exchanging our hard-earned (given) food stamps for change and then bought Dad's audio tapes. Mission accomplished. Except, on our way out of town, we passed by the local theater.

"Whattya think? Wanna go?" my brother asked. "It's *Return of the Jedi!*"

"Yes!" I exclaimed. We had just seen Star Wars a few months prior on our thirteen inch black and white television. It had been on network TV on a Friday night and it captured our imagination! I couldn't believe we were going to have a chance at seeing the latest Star Wars movie in the theater! We walked up to the box office and checked out the start times and the costs. The movie started at 7:15 p.m. and cost three dollars and twenty-five cents. Lucky for us, it was about 6:30 p.m. and we had a bit over seven dollars and some change left. Well, Dad said we could use the change on whatever we wanted and this definitely constituted what we wanted!

We purchased our tickets and snuck the candy in that we had purchased earlier in the day. This was the second time I had ever watched a movie in a theater. I was mesmerized. The theater seats, the lighting, and the stereo speakers were all so enveloping. The evocative smell of fresh popcorn smothered in real butter and tossed heavily with salt was delectable. We didn't have enough money left for popcorn but that didn't matter. I was in heaven.

"A long time ago in a galaxy far, far away..."

For over two hours, we watched furry little ewoks, laser beams, and fighter planes racing through the stars. The battle for the galactic empire was underway and we joined them as we sat there in our safe little seats. By the end of the movie, Lord Vader (Luke's father) had joined his mentors, Obi-wan and Yoda in the afterlife. As spirits, they joined in the party, celebrating both the destruction of the latest Death Star and hope of peace. All was right in the galaxy. We walked out of that theater and couldn't stop talking about how incredible that experience was. We had just seen *Return of the Jedi* in the theater!

As we exited the building though, reality hit fast. It was close to 9:30 p.m. and the sunlight was fading quickly. After a long day of buying, biking, and defeating an evil empire, we were still fifteen miles from home with darkness quickly approaching. There was nothing left to do though, since cell phones hadn't been invented yet.

We jumped on our bikes and started home. It was cool that evening and the air brushed through our hair and past our sleeveless tank tops and shorts. We tried not to pay the cool air any attention though since we were in such a hurry. Our main concern was getting home.

"We are in so much trouble!" my brother yelled, "hurry up!" Of course, he was so much faster than me, and his bike was bigger than mine.

"I'm going as fast as I can! I'm freezing!" I exclaimed. The truth was, I was so worried about what kind of trouble we were going to be in getting home so late. I just wanted to be home right now. But, we rode and rode and rode into the dark, black night on the edge of the two-lane highway toward our impending death. It was another one of those times where I didn't know if they were going to be genuinely concerned about where we were so late at night after sending us out in the morning, or were they going to execute us upon arrival. My assumption was more the latter.

As we rode, we didn't really even know how late it was getting since neither one of us had a watch. Up ahead, I saw a light. I was hoping it was the beginning of our town. I had no idea how long we had left until we made it back home, but it felt like we had ridden forever. As we approached the light, it became clear that it was a gas station. I was glad for at least some semblance of civilization. We pulled into the gas station, hoping to find out how late it was and find out how far we had left. We whipped our bikes into the Sinclair station quickly, parked them on the curb outside and hastily approached the door to enter. Out walked a middle-aged couple that reminded me of my parents and our impending doom. We noticed a clock behind the register.

It was 11:30 p.m.! We were definitely dead, if we ever made it home. Worse than that, we found out we still had about four miles left to go.

"Let's go!" my brother yelled as he quickly exited the building. I wasn't sure how much further I could go. I was tired. I was scared. I was cold. I definitely questioned whether it was all worth it. Certainly, my brother thought so. He was neither tired, nor cold, nor scared. Big brothers have that sort of supreme confidence. This was *my* big brother and he was definitely one of my heroes! I followed along as quickly as I could and we pedaled our way out of the station and back onto that two-lane highway.

About a half mile down the road, a car slowed as we passed it in the opposite direction. I didn't know what we were going to do. My dad and I had been hitchhiking before, so I assumed and hoped someone was about to offer us a ride. I was also a bit petrified. I had never accepted a ride from a stranger without my parents. As the car approaching came to a complete stop, I heard my mom's voice.

"Jimmy?! Shawn?! Is that you?!?" My mom's voice pierced the cold darkness. I was so relieved! Not only we were going to get a ride home the rest of the way, but I didn't have to worry about it being from a complete stranger, not knowing what to do. We were saved! I also noticed that Dad was not with her. We were safe! For now. We happily jumped off our bikes, tossed them in the trunk and jumped in the car.

"Are you boys okay?!" Mom asked. "We've been worried sick about you!"

"Yeah," my brother said. "It just took longer than we thought. We had difficulty getting all the money we needed for Dad's tapes and we got the last tapes that were left!" he lied.

"Genius," I thought. My brother was a genius. He made it seem like our predicament was due to Dad's mission, not our foolish choice to stay and watch a late night movie with a fifteen mile drive home afterward and no way to call. My mom bought it and we didn't die that night; mostly because she was able to convince my dad our story was true. My brother got us through that harrowing adventure. He had a way of doing that which was one of the reasons he was always a hero of mine.

Back to the story at hand – we finished packing the car and Jimmy still had not shown up yet.

"Let's go. Get in the d*mn car!" my dad yelled. We all piled in. Shannon, my youngest brother at the time, sat up front on the cooler with Mom and Dad. My younger sister, Shelby and

I laid down in the back of the car wondering what was happening. We didn't know where we were going. We didn't know where Jimmy was. We left town and drove to Colorado, not stopping to pick Jimmy up anywhere. *Would we get left behind next?* I wondered as we made that trip. *Where was my brother, my hero?* We lost Jimmy.

This was the last time Jimmy ever lived at home. I missed him dearly. We lost many things by moving so often, but my brother was never one of the things I thought we would leave behind. It was beginning to take a toll on me and I was beginning to lose hope for a normal life. This latest move and loss of my brother took place just four years after I hoped we were able to leave my dad behind.

Chapter 5

Loogootee Pt 1 (1980)

New York, New York—the town so nice, they named it twice. That's what they say. Well, this was Loogootee, Indiana (pronounced Luh-go-tee). The town so nice, we lived there thrice.

First, while I was in the second grade. Next, while I was in third grade. And lastly, while I was in the fifth grade. This was, small town, southern Indiana at it's finest – the home of Jack Butcher, all-time winningest high school basketball coach in state history. It lived and breathed the kind of small town basketball straight out of the movie Hoosiers. It wasn't Hickory (or Milan, for that matter), but it may as well have been. It was the kind of small town that John Cougar Mellencamp sang about in his popular song, *Small Town* (his small town was actually just a little bit over an hour away.) Everyone knew everyone and was involved in each other's business.

Four years before we left my brother Jimmy, our first endeavor living in Loogootee was in a hotel. We arrived on a bus after hitchhiking our entire belongings and five kids from New Mexico. We moved into an early twentieth century style hotel where all the rooms were connected inside with an open lobby. There was a large staircase in the center that led up to the second and third floors. Those floors had large expansive balconies that opened into the lobby area. Beautiful hand railings stretched out along the balconies overlaying the lobby. The lobby area was filled with ancient (or antique, depending on your view) furniture. The hallway was filled with turn-of-the-century wallpaper that was supposed to "pretty up the walls." The entire place could have been considered antique or simply, just old. It was no longer in its original glory. At one point, this hotel, in its heyday, was magnificent and expensive. Now it was old, decrepit and cheap.

I'm not sure how we could even afford to live in this hotel. More than likely, my dad's skills got us in good there. When I say my dad's skills, I mean his ability to talk to people. My dad was primarily a physical laborer his whole life. Right out of high school, he joined the Marines during the Vietnam conflict. He loved my mom and they wanted to get married. The military draft was being implemented and my dad expected to be drafted. He wanted some choice in the matter, so he went down to the recruiting office and joined the Marines. He wasn't sure what was in his future, but he knew he wasn't going to college so he decided to join the military.

My mom's parents weren't too excited about this as you might imagine. My mom and dad wanted to get married and their future son-in-law joined the Marines during a time of war. This was not exactly a recipe for a long, lasting marriage. It was more like a recipe for a "Dear John" letter or the inevitable "next of kin" death notification for his parents and would-be wife. My dad decided a pregnancy might force the hands of their conservative parents. Mom didn't have the gumption to tell him she didn't agree with the idea and found herself pregnant shortly thereafter. Societal pressures, as they were, ensured they got married before my dad went off to war.

Dad was assigned as a supply man in the Marines. His physical labor began. My dad was one of the smartest people I've ever met. I'm sure his teachers had said more than once, "if only he applied himself!"

The Marine Corps and the Vietnam war messed my dad up forever. While my dad was always a bit of a rebellious child, he was adopted shortly after birth and never felt loved since his mom gave him up for adoption. My grandparents adopted him when they were in their early forties. He grew up with what many of us would think of as grandparents in an era where that wasn't normal, particularly among the Christian, suburban type. My dad drank all of a six-pack of beer his entire time in high school. He was forced to wear khaki pants and button up dress shirts to his public high school in Griffith, Indiana.

While my dad didn't experience the horrors of actual battle in Vietnam, he was subjected to the fear and uncertainty of people dying all around him. I remember Dad's story of when he had the opportunity to leave. At the end of his tour, he was offered an opportunity to fly out on a helicopter carrying a bunch of dead bodies or wait for the next flight. While the morbid idea of flying out with these young, dead men wasn't a thrilling idea, it was better than the alternative; waiting and potentially being one of them. My dad flew out of Vietnam with the bodies of friends and other servicemen. This was the time in my dad's life where he began drinking and periodically smoking marijuana. Believe it or not, those forms of self-medication were fairly available to our young servicemen in Vietnam.

I imagine my dad was always an emotional man. I definitely got that from him. He simply felt life at an extreme level and then struggled with how to handle that in any sort of positive or healthy manner. He also lived in an era that didn't understand emotions nor how to handle them in any sort of therapeutic manner. Post-traumatic stress disorder (PTSD) wasn't even a thing yet. Counseling for my dad's insecurities related to being given up for adoption wasn't an idea worth pursuing. Instead, self-medication of drinking and drugs, along with the emerging era of "if it feels good, do it" shaped my dad's early twenties. The lyrics of Dad's favorite rock music of the sixties and seventies reinforced many of these same ideas.

I was born in Oceanside, California or more precisely, Camp Pendleton. My parents lived off-base in Fallbrook, but I was born in the Naval Hospital on base. We weren't there very long as my dad was let go about seven months later from the Marines after eight years of service for being overweight. He wasn't severely overweight, but it was enough for the Marines. His weight hadn't changed much during that time. He was always a little heavy. It didn't matter as much while war was being waged in foreign lands, but after the Vietnam war was over, it was time to cut back and his weight was the easy way for them to do that. The consistent paycheck and solid income that he had earned during those years was gone. The hope of making a career out of the military and possibly retiring after twenty years of service disappeared.

All hope was not yet lost though because the steel mills in northern Indiana were booming at the time. My parents moved back to Griffith, Indiana where they were from and grandpa helped Dad get a financially solid job at the local steel mill where he had retired. Later they moved to Hobart Township where they were able to buy their first house. About three years later, the steel mills started to close as cars were increasingly being made of lighter and cheaper materials. My dad went through a period of nearly a year where he was laid off, was able to go back to work and then laid off again. This happened multiple times over that year, until finally, my dad gave up on the steel mills.

This began our life of moving as my dad began to look for work. I had only moved three times in three years at this point. His deep-seated emotional problems and alcoholism created chaos everywhere we went. It was simply easier to leave his problems behind, back in the late seventies and eighties. He didn't have to pay his bills. They didn't follow him from state to state. There was always some landlord who was willing to help us out or let us move in without a deposit. These were my dad's real skills. *He had the gift of gab and could talk anyone into anything*, I thought. I saw him as a master manipulator though, not a salesman, but a manipulator.

My dad was not only an alcoholic, but he had two other accompanying behaviors that terrorized our lives. When he drank, he would often drive. Sometimes he was driving while he was drinking, other times he drove after he drank. He considered himself a better driver when he drank, he tried to convince us (and probably himself) because he drove slower and was more aware of his surroundings as he kept an eye out for cops. The second issue was his anger got the best of him, *particularly* when he drank and he could get pretty violent. My dad wasn't a big fan of guns and never wanted to own one. He knew his limitations in one sense, that if he ever would have owned a gun, he wouldn't be able to control himself when he got drunk and angry. Dad got drunk quite often and was physically abusive with Mom and sometimes with us kids, as well. Probably worse yet for me, he was always verbally and emotionally abusive.

We only lived in that hotel in Loogootee for a week or two when my dad was stopped by the police after leaving a bar, highly intoxicated. He was arrested and put in jail. My mom saw her way out and left him that very night. She was always scared to leave him. Like many abused wives, she was afraid that he would find her and probably kill her and us. She was so fearful of that, but didn't know what to do about it. That night she found the courage and she gathered us all up in the dark cloud of the evening as if it was concealing our departure. We left my dad behind in his drunken state in jail to fend for himself and we were finally freed from his reign of terror. We drove back up toward northern Indiana and Mom found sanctuary for us in a battered women's shelter in Crawfordsville, Indiana. We hid out there for a couple of months hoping and praying he wouldn't find us.

A couple of months later, (once we felt safe and that my dad wasn't returning) we moved back near my mom's family in Portage, Indiana. We rented a house in this small, suburban type city. Life was good. We had finally settled and were living a normal life. I have some pretty fond memories of these nine months in Portage. We lived in a one-story, brick, ranch duplex that was situated next to others just like siblings. It had a nice yard out front and some area parks for the kids to run and have fun like we all used to do. It was all so serene.

Terri, my oldest sister by six years, fell in love with REO Speedwagon's, "Hi Infidelity" album. We spent many days singing *Take it on the Run* together using her hairbrush as a microphone and enjoying the music. Terri had this bright red hair and such a fun, enthusiastic attitude. She had freckles spotting her whole body as numerous as the stars in the sky. Some people complain about this type of complexion, being red-haired and full of freckles, but she wore it well! She was so social and made music so much fun. She was so innocent in life and took things as they came. She was usually the one to get all of us kids together to have some sort of singing or dancing contest to the latest hits.

Jimmy, my older brother by four years, had a Green Machine. A Green Machine was the ultimate type of Big Wheel. A Big Wheel was a road ready, type of plastic tricycle built for older kids of six to ten years old. I always looked up to him in many ways, and him having the ultimate Big Wheel was just one more reason. The Green Machine was unique in its lime green and black color, but also in its design. Big Wheels typically had a pedal system on the front tire, but not the Green Machine. It had a peg on the front wheel for our feet, but it had these hand pedals of sorts that we moved back and forth like we were rowing a canoe, rotating each arm back and forth. We could build up some incredible speed and do some great peel-outs. I had a normal Big Wheel and it was fun too, but not like his Green Machine. We would race our Big Wheels up and down our street, sidewalk and driveway.

We used to play all over our neighborhood, running to and fro with our friends. Although I was only seven and my brother was eleven, we were free to run and enjoy the neighborhood. "Be home by dark," my mom would say and we were, out of respect and appreciation for our mom.

Mom was a beautiful, quiet, loving woman. She was kind and took good care of us. We knew she wanted the best for us, even if she didn't always know how to make that happen. She parented in a hands-free kind of way, but provided what we needed in boundaries, food and support if we came asking for it. She was always a hard worker. In a time when not all moms worked. She worked on and off through the years based on our need and ability to do so without needing to pay a babysitter to watch us. During our time in Portage, she had gotten a job paying insurance claims for MetLife. It was a decent job and allowed us to live in what I remember as a pristine neighborhood. Terri was thirteen so when we were home from school, she was able to watch us while Mom worked. She was a fairly good pseudo-mom too when Mom wasn't around. She also treated us well and gave us freedom to explore the neighborhood.

We even had the chance to go to church while we lived there. We attended a small Christian church not far from our house. One week, they gave me this great children's Bible and I cherished it. It had a picture of Jesus on the front, holding a lamb. I don't know if I ever read it, but it was meaningful to me at the time. As I look back, I fondly remember that first Bible. This was really the only time my family ever attended church when we weren't there for the sole purpose of a handout.

My dad, the master manipulator, had a way of getting help from pastors and churches too. Most of my experience with church in my childhood was my dad bumming something from them like gas, money, or our next meal. We attended once or twice as part of my dad's method, but only when it seemed necessary. But, here in this serene community, we were able to truly participate as members, attending regularly, not as bums seeking a handout.

If I had been able to live this life from that point forward, this story would not have been written. But, it didn't last long. I always had this fear that someday, my dad would show up and ruin our lives again. I was afraid that he would take away this pleasant, normal living experience we had created without him. Then, one day, when I was out riding my Big Wheel by myself, I spied my dad sitting in a car across the street. I pretended I didn't notice and kept riding around. Not long after, I went inside hoping he didn't see me.

The next night after dinner, my mom told us all to stay inside and she went out front. We looked out the window as we saw her approach the vehicle, then walk around to get in on the passenger side. They sat in that car for what seemed like an eternity. I prayed that Mom would not fall for whatever he was trying to tell her. I just knew he was trying to get her back. I imagined, in his master manipulator ways, he was talking her into taking him back. Hours later, my mom came back into the house with my dad. I could tell they had been crying and I instinctively knew this new life we had found was over.

Things quickly went back to *our* normal. We packed the car and moved to our next temporary location. I lost the life I had hoped to live.

We moved a couple of times in the next three months, as far as Missouri. My dad's best friend from high school lived there and was now a pastor. He performed their second wedding ceremony while we were there. Unfortunately for us, they were able to restart their life together, which meant that we were back on the road again. Sadly, we actually returned to Loogootee for one of the biggest losses of my entire life.

Chapter 6

Loogootee Pt 2 (1981)

We moved into a run-down trailer park that was really no trailer park at all. In its heyday, this trailer park may have housed ten to twelve trailers. There were about three or four that were still lived in while we were there; the rest of the spaces were vacant. When we turned right into the trailer park off the small town street, we rounded the bend on a dirt road with a lot of overgrown trees, bushes, and tall grass. The area was not well manicured, as lawns and vegetation go. As we turned right, there was a row of trailers on our right and typical southern Indiana woods on our left. Junk or maybe just abandoned cars were strewn throughout the vacant lots and left over trash was spread around in front of people's trailers.

I couldn't believe we were returning to the town where Mom had finally left Dad. They had gotten back together and remarried in Missouri just a couple of months earlier. We literally returned to the misery that we came from. However, our experience, at first, wasn't that bad. Dad wasn't drinking and we began to enjoy our small town, early eighties life. *Wonder Woman* was our favorite TV show, along with the *Six Million Dollar Man*. Terri, Jimmy, and I rode our bikes all over town. It was a safe place and no one ever questioned our freedom to run and go as we pleased even though we were only fourteen, twelve, and eight respectively. Jimmy and I loved to go into the woods and explore.

"What the h*ll is that?!!" I screamed.

"Those are tadpoles, you idiot," my brother explained. We had found a small pool of water in the woods that was filled with what seemed like hundreds of tadpoles. They looked like oversized worms, squirming and flapping about in the small puddle of water. They were disgusting, but mesmerizing. *What the heck are those?* I wondered even though my brother just told me.

"What's a tadpole???" I asked, truly not knowing.

"It's a baby frog, dildo!" my brother's friend said. "How did your brother get so stupid?" he asked Jimmy. Jimmy just laughed. I was used to that. I always looked up to my older brother and admired him, but he didn't always treat me the best; nor care about my feelings. He did care about me and he protected me too. He fought in my honor more than once when I was getting picked on. My feelings, he didn't seem to care so much about, but then again, he was much less emotional. The small pool of tadpoles were disgusting and I was done looking at them. I was afraid one of them was going to hop up into my lap or touch me somehow. For a young boy, I sure didn't care much for the creepy, crawlies.

"We should keep some of them! Watch them grow into full blown frogs," my brother suggested.

"What do you mean?" I asked, still not fully comprehending.

"Tadpoles are just baby frogs," he explained. "As they grow, they develop legs and their bodies change shape. They may look funny right now, but they will look like a normal frog in just a few weeks!" he explained. I was dumbfounded. *How will those disgusting, little slimy things turn into frogs?* I wondered. *Each and every one of them?*

We ran back to our trailer and found a large clear mixing bowl that we could use as a "fish tank" to keep them as pets. My brother took that bowl and scooped up four or five of them, being sure to keep some of that puddle water. We took them back to the house and put them up on a dresser in our shared bedroom. We borrowed some cat food from the neighbors, crumbled it up and fed them periodically. That was it. That's the extent of how we cared for them.

Later that day, when we were riding our bikes on the road in our rundown trailer park, we found a snake. Well, we found part of a snake. It was about an inch in diameter and eight to ten inches long. It looked like it had been run over by a car, then run over by a bike, then run over by a lawn mower. It was smashed and cut up to the point that *nothing could live through that,* I thought. We were all a bit freaked out and disgusted by it, but I guess that's what boys did. We took home tadpoles to live on our dresser and fiddled around with half-dead snakes. We played with that snake, but from afar using a long stick to poke and prod it.

"What the h*ll?!" my brother's friend yelled as that snake started to slither around. That snake started moving as if it had come back from the dead like a zombie. We all jumped back, but then Jimmy and his friend burst out laughing. I was freaked out. That half-dead or zombie snake had literally moved around and slithered as if nothing happened to it.

"These snakes can slither around and move for up to twenty four hours after they die," my brother explained. He was so freaking smart. When it came to guy stuff, Jimmy knew everything.

"What? So... it.... *is*... dead?" I asked quizzically.

"Of course, look at it." He poked and prodded it. It slithered and moved a bit, but it was terribly cut up and smashed. I didn't know what to think, but Jimmy knew everything so I trusted him. Then my brother reached for his pocket knife and decided that he was going to prove his point. He was a bit afraid I could tell because he wouldn't just grab that *dead* snake, but he took his pocket knife and started cutting into the middle of it. After several minutes of playing with his meat, like it was the first steak he had ever eaten, he was able to cut through it. Two snake halves literally laid there on the road and both parts were squirming around.

"That's disgusting! I'm out of here," I proclaimed and then rode off on my bike by myself. I loved to hang out with my brother, but I wasn't going to stay there. That snake freaked me out. I rode my bike around the neighborhood for a bit and then headed home. I passed by the city pool on my way that was near the bowling alley. It looked like a great place to swim, but summer was over and even though it was a Sunday, the weather had gotten too cool to swim. It was kind of neat living that close to the pool, but we never got to use it since summer was already over and we weren't there long enough for the following season. When I arrived home, I went inside to watch television.

We had a great thirteen inch color television! I'm still amazed when I look back and think about all we didn't have, but somehow we always had money for TVs, stereos and a VCR or seven. I turned on the television by pulling the knob and turning the channel to 45. Our TV had two channel dials. Many of our favorite channels with kids shows were on UHF so you had to turn the top knob to "U" and the bottom knob to 45. On popped one of my favorite shows, *Buck Rogers in the 25th Century*.

I plopped down and watched by myself. Watching TV was certainly one of my favorite past times. Buck took me to another world. I didn't really notice how quirky or cheesy it was at the time. Or, at least, I didn't care. Twiggy was the best friend I never had. He went with me no matter what town we lived in. I suppose that was one of the greatest consistencies I did have in my life. No matter where we lived, I always had a TV and the shows didn't change. I could stay in touch with Buck Rogers, the Million Dollar Man, Wonder Woman, and my friends on Gilligan's island whether we lived in Indiana, New Mexico, California, Colorado, Illinois or wherever else the road took us. Gilligan's silly antics would be there to make me laugh and feel a little bit better about life.

TV also kept us from doing our chores which often got us into hot trouble too. In our house, the kids were most responsible to keep the house clean. We all had chores and typically, we would get a small allowance. My dad liked the idea of us learning how to earn our pay, while at the same time keeping the house clean. We didn't do a great job though. After school, one of our favorite programs to come home and watch was *Wonder Woman*. I can't tell you how often we came home to watch Lynda Carter lassoing up some lying guy with her truth-telling rope. We got so caught up in the story that we never got around to cleaning our trailer, like one particular afternoon in Loogootee.

We were watching one of our favorite shows when suddenly all was quiet as the programming switched to a commercial. We heard the sound of tires pulling up and pebbles being thrown about when my parents' car entered the driveway. Terri, Jimmy and I looked at each other in startled fear. We were motionless for a split second and then all of the sudden, we sprang into action.

Mom and Dad were home and we had spent all afternoon watching our shows. We hadn't cleaned the house nor done any chores. We knew it was over. We knew Dad was going to kill us. Jimmy pushed the knob to turn off the TV and we all sprinted to our cleaning spots. Terri went to the kitchen to straighten it up. Jimmy ran to the bathroom to see what was out of order. I started grabbing anything lying about in the living room and threw it in our bedroom, which was right next to the living room.

Dad entered first. His large, physical presence was enough to frighten us into scrambling to do our chores. He was nearly six foot tall and about two hundred and twenty five pounds at this time. Since he worked manual labor, he wasn't skinny and he had a large beer belly. His thick, but stringy hair fell out from under his trucker ball cap and was scraggly, hanging long beyond his neck line. His hair was a deep brown, but had strong hints of red that was representative of his temper. He had a few freckles too, if you looked closely. This wasn't the time for that. He was angry.

"What the h*ll was going on in here?!" he yelled. We all just quickly and quietly went about our business of trying to complete thirty minutes of chores in sixty seconds. Dad placed his hand on the television, which was by the front door that entered directly into the living room.

"Why is the TV hot?!" he yelled. Nobody wanted to say anything. We just kept scurrying, hoping he wasn't coming to us first. I grabbed two pillows that we brought in from our bedroom to the living room floor to watch TV. I darted toward our bedroom with them. Dad was quicker. He snatched the back of my shirt as I went by and grabbed me up like I was a fly he snatched out of the air, like Mr. Miyagi with his chopsticks in *The Karate Kid*.

"I don't know!" I cried, hoping he would just let it go. I knew he wouldn't. His other hand came around and smacked me on the back of the head.

"Why is there crap all over the living room?!" he exclaimed, not really asking now. He knew why. He knew we had been watching TV and ignoring our chores. My dad hated coming home from a hard day's work to a dirty house. He probably hated that more than anything. *Maybe we drove him to drink*, I used to think. That's the kind of thing an eight year old thinks. "You've been watching TV after school and you lazy b*st*rds haven't done a thing!" I prayed my dad would let me go and I could squirm away to my bedroom.

Suddenly, I did drop.

"Terri! What the h*ll have you been doing?!" Terri had been quickly trying to clean up the kitchen and get the dishes started making it look as if she had been working for a while on it, but now she immediately started crying. She knew she was about to get beat. "Get over here! Where's Jim? Jimmy get in here!" Jimmy came flying around the corner from down the hallway where the bathroom was. "What the h*ll is that smell?!" Dad yelled.

I hadn't noticed it before, but all of the sudden it hit me. The tadpoles. Jimmy slid past my dad toward the bedroom. As he reached his hand inside our bedroom door on top of the dresser, he retracted the clear mixing bowl with the tadpoles in it. They were all laying upside down with X's across their eyes signifying they were dead. The smell of dead tadpoles permeated the living room now. I was even more grossed out than I was when I saw them in a puddle in the woods. They had these little baby legs now and I could tell they had been morphing into frogs before they died an early death. My brother, near the front door now tossed them out; water and all.

"All three of you, on the couch!" he yelled.

We knew what that meant. Dad was about to take off his belt and beat us with it. Terri's crying grew louder and more dramatic. Jimmy just quietly went over to the couch, ready to take it like a man. I, on the other hand, started crying too. I was so afraid of what was about to happen.

"Jim! What's going on?!" Mom pleaded. Mom was now walking in the door holding the hand of my younger sister, Shelby. She was three years old and holding my younger brother, Shannon in her other arm. He was only about a year old. Mom was trying to figure out what was going on as she was just now getting in the house.

"These pieces of sh*t have been lying around watching TV when they were supposed to be doing their chores! We work hard all day to put food on the table and give them a place to live and this is the thanks we get!" he yelled.

Somehow Dad never got the fact that we were kids and should have expected at some level for us to be irresponsible. Plus, he had his way of fixing things he didn't like. He got angry. He yelled. He belittled. He got physical. Then he drank to try and get over it. Or it started with drinking and led to the rest. It was all a pretty vicious cycle.

I imagine he struggled with many of the feelings of anger, sadness, and frustration that many parents struggle with, but he was also weighed down by many other experiences from his past. Many parents work long hard days and have expectations and responsibilities for their children. They put food on the table and the children do their assigned chores. For me, it was his overreaction and unrealistic expectations of perfection. All I knew at the time — I was experiencing a living hell.

Terri, Jimmy and I faced the couch, put our knees on the floor and bent over the seat with our elbows on the couch cushions side by side. Dad got me first with his belt.

One.

Two.

Three.
Four.
Five.

I lost it. I balled as if it was the most extreme pain I had ever experienced. My father was beating me for what seemed like such an insignificant thing. I mean, we would have done our chores eventually, especially once he got home and told us to do them. We just didn't do it because we got caught up in being kids and watching TV. I didn't know when or if he was going to stop. Terri and Jimmy were laying next to me, both now sobbing because they knew they were next.

"Stop, stop," Terri cried. She was just hoping he would stop it all, but she could also see that I couldn't handle it.

"Shut the h*ll up!" Dad screamed. "Go to your room, Shawn!" he continued. I launched myself off the floor and darted into my room and around the doorway. As I did, I closed the door behind me and hit my bed. My face went deep into my pillow as I continued to sob uncontrollably. I could still hear Dad's belt smacking Jimmy's backside.

One. Two. Three. Four. Five. Six. Seven, Eight. Nine. Ten. Eleven. Twelve. Thirteen. Fourteen. Fifteen. Sixteen. Seventeen. Eighteen. Nineteen. Twenty. Twenty one. Twenty two. Twenty three. Twenty four. Twenty five. Twenty six. Twenty seven. Twenty eight. Twenty nine. Thirty. Thirty one. Thirty two. Thirty three. Thirty four. Thirty five. Thirty six. Thirty seven. Thirty eight. Thirty nine. Fourty.

"Get the h*ll up and go to your room!" he yelled at Jimmy. Jimmy, sobbing and hurt, scraped himself up and hobbled to join me in our room. I could hear Shelby and Shannon crying now along with the rest of us even though they were too young to really understand what was happening.

"Jim, stop!" my mom yelled. Sometimes, she tried to advocate for us. Sometimes, she sat back, afraid of what he might do to her *or us* if she did try to intervene.

"They did this to themselves! If they want to be lazy pieces of sh*t, they can pay the piper!" he yelled. Suddenly, I could hear through the wall again as Terri started to cry out.

"Stop, stop!" she screamed as she cried uncontrollably.

One. Two. Three. Four. Five. Six. Seven, Eight. Nine. Ten. Eleven. Twelve. Thirteen. Fourteen. Fifteen. Sixteen. Seventeen. Eighteen. Nineteen. Twenty. Twenty one. Twenty two. Twenty three. Twenty four. Twenty five. Twenty six. Twenty seven. Twenty eight. Twenty nine. Thirty. Thirty one. Thirty two. Thirty three. Thirty four. Thirty five. Thirty six. Thirty seven. Thirty eight. Thirty nine. Fourty.

The room went silent. I heard rustling as I imagined Terri getting up and going to her room to put her face in her pillow and cry herself to sleep that night, just like me.

"Jim, they're just kids!" Mom pleaded again.

"They are old enough to know better and be responsible to do their chores. They know better than to come home and watch TV when they are supposed to be cleaning this sh*thole up." My dad made his way to the fridge, opened up a twelve pack and pulled one of his cans of Schlitz out.

"Snickt, pftt, sizzle," the can spoke. That sound immediately began to temper Dad's anger a bit. He leaned his head back and upward as he poured a good portion into his mouth and down his throat without hardly tasting it. Apparently, Dad had started drinking again. Mom fled with Shelby and Shannon back to Terri's room where she tried to help the two younger ones stop crying while consoling Terri.

"Get your *ss back out here and make dinner!" Dad scolded Mom. Mom was always compliant, particularly when Dad was this angry and violent.

Who knew what he was capable of doing?! she wondered. She went back out to the kitchen and living room to try to calm Dad down while making dinner and getting him another beer. There was a bit of heated discussion, some back and forth, but most of it was coming from Dad. Mom was careful to not say anything that might keep him riled up. Dad spouted his anger and drank his beer. Eventually, Mom finished dinner and he ate. Then he grabbed the rest of his twelve pack and went out to the car. The car engine roared back up and he pulled out of the driveway leaving us all shriveled up messes. Our hope of a better life was gone.

I can only imagine how Terri and Jimmy felt. They received much worse than I did. Jimmy always seemed to handle it so much better. He was less emotional. He was stronger. He was smarter. Terri on the other hand, was always quick to cry. She was always very emotional, much more like me. I imagine that's why she left first.

Chapter 7

Loogootee Pt 2b (1981)

The next day, when we woke up to go to school, Mom and Dad were already gone with Shelby and Shannon. The house had returned to peace. Mom and Dad both worked at the local turkey processing plant; killing and processing turkeys for human consumption. They had to get up early and leave before any of us were awake for school. Mom took Shelby and Shannon to a babysitter since the rest of us were in school. We were left to fend for ourselves in the morning; eating, dressing and running to catch the bus, which typically wasn't a problem.

Today though, we were all mentally and emotionally recovering from the aftermath of the night before. *Why did Dad hate us so much? Why couldn't we just do what we were supposed to do? Why was he so violent?* We all spent the morning getting ready, trying to process and comprehend what we just went through and having to face the day at school.

Surprisingly, we all adjusted fairly well to school despite the challenges of our lives. School was a fairly positive experience for me. The teachers were typically nice and cared about me. They were kind and helpful. When I messed up, they didn't cuss at me, tell me I was a piece of crap and smack me upside the head. The worst case scenario was, I got sent to the principal and had to sit outside his office for a bit, then ended up talking to the secretary or counselor nearby, if I talked to anyone at all.

This day, however, none of us were ready to go face all that school had for us. We were experiencing our own version of PTSD. These shows provided the fantastical escape that we needed.

Terri took her bowl of cereal, sat in front of the TV, turned it on and started watching *The Bozo Show*. I grabbed my own bowl and joined her. Jimmy was already sitting on the couch with his bowl. We all sat there in the memory of our misery, eating the bagged puffed wheat with as much sugar as it took to taste like *Sugar Smacks* and let Bozo the Clown help us forget about our real lives.

We laughed slightly and stayed glued to the TV all the way up to the *Grand Prize Game* where each of us imagined we got a ping pong ball to toss in each bucket. We imagined participating in the fun as they progressed through the buckets, starting with the closest of six buckets, tossing the ball into and hopefully staying in each bucket, working our way to the grand prize. We envisioned earning the reward — a grand prize of extreme proportions — which I imagined as getting away from Dad and living a normal life.

The show ended at the conclusion of the *Grand Prize Game* and the next show started. It was a rerun of *Bewitched*, which I loved. I looked at the clock and started to worry that we had already missed the bus, but Terri and Jimmy were in charge while my parents were gone, so I figured they knew what they were doing. These TV shows took me into another world and allowed me to escape, if for a moment, to a better place and time. Once *Bewitched* ended, a rerun of *The Jeffersons* came on. I didn't care much for that show. It seemed more like a show for adults. *Of course,* I wondered, *that's probably because kids are supposed to be at school.*

"Uh, are we going to school or what?" I asked, letting the words hang in the air.

"Not today. Let's just stay home and watch TV," Terri responded without much fanfare. That sounded just fine to me. I wasn't much in the mood for school and I was still a bit of a mess from the night before. Terri turned the channel and found, *The Price is Right* and we all continued to play along in our heads imagining our own prizes. After *The Price is Right* was over, Terri got up and turned the TV off.

"Let's go," she said.

"What?" I asked. There was no way I was going to school now. We were hours late and it was a long walk. I just knew we would get in even more trouble for arriving at school late. I couldn't do it.

"We are going to get in bigger trouble than last night if Mom and Dad find out we skipped school. We'll just tell them we missed the bus. As long as we go to school, we'll be fine," Terri explained.

"No way!" I said. "You said we could stay home. I would be so embarrassed to go into school late. They will see right through us!" I pleaded.

"We have to go." Jimmy stated plainly.

Terri and Jimmy did their chores meticulously, cleaning the bathroom and kitchen — knowing they couldn't let a repeat of last night happen again. They even helped clean the living room of everything including our dishes from that morning. If

Dad saw dirty dishes in the living room, he would literally kill us. That was always a pet peeve of his. Dirty dishes in the living room or bedroom meant bugs. Bugs meant a dirty house. He wasn't having that. No bugs. No dirty dishes. No way. We all cleaned the living room before we left, but I was way too embarrassed and refused to go.

"Fine," Terri said. "We'll leave without you. Your life is in your hands." Terri and Jimmy exited the trailer and started to walk to school, which was about a mile and a half away. I couldn't believe it. First, they said we were staying home. Then, they tried to take it back. It was way too late for that. We were already so late! There was no way I was going to school more than two hours late, plus we would have to walk a mile and a half!

I turned the TV back on and tried to find something to watch. I flipped between a morning show, two soap operas and another game show that I didn't like. Nothing. Now I was stuck home alone, skipping school while my brother and sister were walking to school without me, the day after I got five swats with the belt. I was so lost and didn't know what to do.

About that time, the front door opened back up and Terri popped her head in.

"Let's go," she said. "Jimmy went on to school, but I couldn't leave you here. If you get caught, I'm dead. I'm responsible for you. Let's go!" she exclaimed. I knew I had to go. No choice, but I still didn't want to. We headed out the door and started walking to school. It was such a long walk and we passed that same bowling alley and city pool that I had always wanted to swim at.

Why can't I just have some sort of a normal life? I wondered as we continued to walk the back way to school. We could have arrived at school a little quicker if we walked the front way, but that would have taken us right down front street by all the business and the cars driving up and down the street at 10:30

in the morning. We continued up the back way and I thought more and more about how embarrassed I was going to be, having to explain why I was late to the teacher and the other kids in class. We still hadn't gone to school here for more than a couple of months and I was pretty shy at this age to begin with. Finally, after we had walked three fourths of the way to school, my mind had gotten the best of me and I changed my mind, again.

"I can't do it. I'm not going to school," I pleaded.

"Yes, you are! We are almost there!" she said.

"No, you can't make me. It's your fault anyway! You said we were staying home!" I cried.

"Fine, go home. I'm going to school. And I'm going to tell the cops you are skipping school," she argued.

Yeah, right, I thought. *She is going to tell the cops. They didn't have cops at schools. She would be lucky to tell the principal. They wouldn't do anything about it. What are they going to do, come get me?!* I thought.

I turned around and started walking back home. Terri went on to school. I walked home wondering if there was any other option. I just couldn't face my teacher or classmates being late. About a half-mile later when I was about half-way home, I heard a car coming down this less frequently used street. I turned to see how far away it was and to move further over to the far side of the street since there were no sidewalks in this particular area. As I careened my head around, I realized the car was a cop.

Are you freaking, kidding me?! I thought. *Nobody ever drives this street and it happens to be a cop!* I hoped he hadn't seen me at this point and I moved over further into the ditch as if to hide my presence. I could hear the car slowing down and I reached down to my shoes as if to pretend I stopped to tie them.

"Hey there, little buddy," the cop called.

"Oh, hi there," I responded.

"You doing alright?" he asked. "Why aren't you in school?"

"Oh, yeah. I, uh, wasn't feeling well today," I explained.

"Oh yeah, then what are you doing out here?" he persisted.

"I started to come to school, but then I felt sick. So, I'm heading home." I was sure he understood that or at least, I hoped he would.

"Well, guess what?" he replied. "Good news. There is a nurse at school to take care of you. Come on, get in my car." I walked up to the passenger door and let myself in. I sheepishly pulled myself into the large front passenger seat. "Don't forget to buckle," he said. I didn't know what my parents would find out, but even after the night before, I was so embarrassed to be going to school late and arriving in a cop car, at that!

I was so angry at my sister. *How could she really go and tell the cops on me?!* She was supposed to look after me. It was her idea to stay home to begin with. Terri was a good older sister. She took care of me, but this just bothered me. Jimmy was also a great older brother, but he took a bit more of a hands off approach, mostly just living his life and leading me or helping me when he was in a position to do so.

Thankfully, I don't remember my parents ever finding out about our arriving to school late or my car ride with a police officer. If they did, maybe Dad just felt bad about the night before, but I doubt it.

A couple of months later, it was nearly time for Christmas. Christmas was a time of irony in our family growing up. Even though Christmas has been celebrated as the birth of Jesus Christ, my dad was anything but religious. He rebelled against that life he grew up with. But we celebrated Christmas to the tee. We always had a large Christmas and we always had tons of presents! Even when we had very little to our name, had just moved or were getting ready to move, we always received a lot of gifts. I suppose the sentimentality of Christmas had a profound effect on Dad and he wanted us to experience the same.

I found out years later that Dad's parents typically sent us money at Christmas because they knew us kids wouldn't get much otherwise. If they didn't know where to find us in a particular year, Dad may have used a bad check or two to pay for it as well. He had a short phase where that got us through when we needed it.

One year though, due to moving or money, we didn't even have a tree. I had colored a tree at school on a piece of paper and brought it home to my parents. They ended up using that colored Christmas tree as our actual tree that year. Not sure why this was the case though, since Dad typically went out in the woods somewhere and cut one down for free. We had a lot of gifts that year too, under a hand-colored tree on paper.

This was the year I figured things out about Santa too.

"Hey, come check this out!" my brother yelled from the bathroom to Terri and I. It was another one of those days after school before my parents came home. While Jimmy was cleaning the bathroom, he found some unwrapped presents in the washing machine.

"Whoah!" I exalted. Jimmy was holding up several toys. There was this great "crash car" that I had really wanted. It was about eight inches long and three inches wide. You put the rubber tires on the floor, pulled back and the car would shoot off down the hallway. As soon as it ran into something; CRASH! The doors, roof, and parts of the car would go flying into pieces. You could then pick them back up and put it back together again.

Jimmy had found a pellet rifle behind the washing machine, still in its box. We knew it was a gift for someone because Dad hated guns. I'm sure his experience in Vietnam had something to do with that. Like Ralphie in *A Christmas Story*, my brother Jimmy had wanted a gun for Christmas. Dad had told him there was no way he was getting a gun because he, himself didn't believe in them. We were sure he wouldn't get a gun, until we found it behind the washing machine. Terri found a box filled with a Lite-Brite machine. She was so happy, even though I thought it was a bit hokey myself. We were all so elated to find what we were getting that year for Christmas. We still hadn't thought too much about who had gotten those gifts for us, we were just happy we were getting them.

Christmas morning finally came around and, like I said, it was a big deal. An eight year old cannot sleep the night before Christmas. It's a well known fact. They simply cannot sleep. We always wanted to go to bed early because that meant we were getting up early and Santa wouldn't come until we were asleep. I imagined, as most eight year olds do, Santa arriving and landing on our trailer. *Would he somehow magically come in through the roof since there was no chimney or did he simply use the front door?* I wasn't sure and I didn't really care that much. I just couldn't wait.

The next morning when we awoke early, Jimmy and I opened our bedroom door and peered into the living room. The tree shone brightly in the early morning darkness. It was surrounded by a large myriad of gifts just waiting to be discovered and unwrapped! We were so excited and our stockings were sitting in front of the tree just waiting to be emptied into our glorious laps. But no one else was up yet.

"What do we do?" I asked Jimmy. "Do we wake them up? Or just wait?"

"I'm not sure. I guess we have to wait," he responded. We walked into the living room and looked around peering all around the tree. There must have been a hundred gifts for us five kids! We looked down at each of the packages trying to figure out whose was whose. We peaked at the top of our stockings, but we didn't dare look inside. We knew we had to wait.

"Let's go see if they are awake," I suggested to Jimmy.

We walked down the back hallway past the bathroom to see if either of the other two bedrooms had any movement or sound. As we arrived to listen in on the doors, we did hear some sound from Terri & Shelby's room. I tapped on the door. Terri flung it open.

"Yes! We were afraid you wouldn't be up," Terri said with Shelby hanging around her leg.

"Santa came!" I exclaimed through a whisper.

"We know! We've been up for a couple of hours," Terri said. "This booger wouldn't let me go back to sleep even if I wanted." She peered down at Shelby, smiling. Terri and Shelby exited the room and came out to the tree and we all gleamed at it and the presents over and over again, just hoping our parents would be up soon and we could tear into the gifts.

Terri, finally had the guts to go tap on their door. She went back to their bedroom door as we all hid around the corner in the kitchen.

"Mom? Dad? Are you up yet?" she whispered. "Santa came!" now a bit more excitedly.

"Yes, honey," Mom replied. "We know. We'll be out in a bit." Mom and Dad came out an eternity later, it seemed. It was probably only ten or fifteen minutes later, but it sure seemed like an eternity. Dad was in a good mood. He brewed coffee, took his cup to the living room and put on Christmas music.

"Now who wants to open the first gift?" he asked with a big smile on his face.

"We still have our stockings to open yet," Terri mentioned.

"Well, go ahead!" Dad said anticipating all of the happiness and joy he would have watching us unload all of the items they had filled them with just a few hours earlier.

It was a great morning! We opened our stockings, which were filled with candy and all kinds of little trinkets and *Hot Wheels*. We were filled with exuberance and joy! Then, came our *Grand Prize Game* where we got to open all of our wrapped gifts that were nestled quietly under the tree. Each of us had quite a few gifts to open, but the most memorable one each of us received, with gift tags clearly marked on them as being directly from Santa, were a "Crash Car" for me, a *Lite-Brite* for Terri and a pellet rifle for Jimmy. We knew what that meant, but we kept it to ourselves not daring to tell our parents, nor Shelby and Shannon.

Later that early afternoon, we had a big dinner complete with turkey AND ham, stuffing, sweet potatoes covered with marshmallows, canned cranberry sauce, fresh homemade bread, pecan AND mincemeat pie! It was glorious. The house was filled with happiness and joy.

Until it wasn't. Mom and Dad got in an argument after dinner. Dad had been drinking for a couple of hours. Finally, the argument erupted into yelling, at which Dad called Terri into the room. As Dad yelled at Terri, it was like seeing a Norman Rockwell painting suddenly erupt into a warzone. It literally felt like stuff was flying, weapons were being shot and the sounds of war were terrorizing our ears and hearts on this wonderful Christmas day. That beautiful morning changed into a horrific afternoon right before our eyes. Dad yelled and Mom tried to calm him. Terri cried and didn't know what to do. One thing led to another and Dad ended up beating Terri with his belt.

She went back to her room and we all hid in ours with our new found loot. We hid away, hoping that it would all go away and be forgotten in a few hours. After an hour or so, I heard Dad yell for Terri to come back out of her room. He yelled and yelled at her and then made her go to the local grocery store and get a newspaper for him. He loved to read the newspaper, particularly on holidays and other days of importance.

Terri left that day to get the paper and that was the last time I saw her. Next thing I knew, we were on the road again to Colorado without Terri. Terri ran away to the authorities because

Dad had beaten her and she was placed in a foster home, not because of the beating (there were no bruises), but because we were moving, Mom later told me. Dad decided he wasn't sticking around to face the law again. This was the same place he had stayed overnight in jail for a DUI when Mom left him just over a year before. He wasn't about to deal with that again.

This was, actually, the *first* time we left behind one of my siblings. We loaded up as quickly as we could and headed on down the road to Sterling, Colorado. Once again, we had lost our hope of a normal life *without* my dad. We had lost hope of a normal life *with* my dad. Now, we lost Terri too. This wasn't the first time Terri ran away, but it was the last. Terri had tried running away just a few years before that when she had cut only half my hair, her boyfriend walked on our pool table and us kids wrecked the car into a tree.

Chapter 8

Dad's beginnings (1947, 1965, 1973 - 1979)

Dad wasn't always like that. He wasn't always violent, loose with his words, and having a propensity to the bottle. He was born in Griffith, Indiana in 1947. His mother had given him up for adoption, presumably because she had been impregnated out of wedlock, in a day and time when that was even less acceptable than when my older sister was born. He was adopted from the hospital a day or two after he was born. His adoptive parents could not have children and finally, when they were in their early forties, they adopted my dad. They adopted his sister a couple of years later.

Surprising to my story, Dad was adopted into a typical, suburban Christian home. His father was an elder in the Methodist church and his mother played the organ. They were good people, but raised their kids like many did at the time. Dad received his own fair share of whippings with the belt and once or twice with grandpa's hands. He was always a difficult child and had to be kept in line much more than his younger sister who got away with a lot as *the favorite*. They were raised in the church and given fairly strict requirements, such as wearing khaki slacks and button up shirts to school. Jeans and t-shirts were a definite no-no. They never hurt for money since his parents were in their forties and his dad was well established in his career by the time they were able to adopt children.

That being said, my dad struggled with three main things growing up. His dad was demanding and physical with him. Because of this and the fact that his (also adopted) sister was rarely disciplined from his perspective, Dad felt unloved and unwanted; both by his adopted parents and, of course, by his biological parents simply because they gave him up at birth. He was a bit rebellious as a teenager, but not too much. In fact, all through high school, Dad says that he drank less than six beers. While he never admitted to believing in God, though that was expected in both his home and his culture, his rebellion was fairly limited during this time.

Mom and Dad both graduated from Griffith High School in 1966 and 1965 respectively. Mom dated Dad's best friend who later became a minister and was the pastor who remarried them after their divorce. They didn't date long though, and obviously Mom ended up with Dad. My parents had planned to get married and start a life together, but then rumblings of a war in southeast Asia could be heard throughout the country.

The Vietnam Conflict really began heating up in 1964 as it relates to the United States' involvement of sending troops into battle. The draft began that same year. Dad turned eighteen in January 1965 and graduated high school that same spring. Mom was a year behind in school, though she was two years younger. They had fallen in love and wanted to spend their lives together. There was a lot of uncertainty with the draft looming so Dad decided to take matters into his own hands. He wanted to have some say in which service he was in and what his job might be, so he joined the United States Marine Corps as a supplyman. With the Vietnam Conflict looming and Dad signed up to go to bootcamp; Mom and Dad decided to get married.

Mom's parents didn't think this was a great idea. They didn't want them to get married, only to have Dad go off to war a few months later. They knew they would all spend countless hours wondering if he was going to be killed and leave Mom a widow at the age of eighteen. They forbid them to be married. They did what I imagine any star-crossed lovers forbidden to be married would do in that day and age. Dad got Mom pregnant.

This forced their parents' hands and as good Christian people, they were manipulated into allowing the marriage. Mom and Dad got married on December 27, 1966. Eight months later, Terri was born. Dad went off to bootcamp and eventually Vietnam.

While he did not see battle as a supplyman, one can only imagine the challenges of being in Vietnam during that time period. Life and death was day to day for both him and his buddy next to him. One of Dad's best friends from high school joined with him on the buddy program and ended up at the Siege of Khe Sanh in early 1968. The Battle of Khe Sanh had produced the largest ratio of US troops killed in Vietnam, though the actual numbers are difficult to agree on or determine. Dad, however, did not have to endure these intense battles, but as one can imagine, it would be a challenge for anyone to manage emotionally.

Dad was always a very emotional person. There is not much dispute about that. Though his hair had just a tinge of red and just a few freckles when you looked close, he was an angry guy with a fiery temper. He was also a very sad young man who felt unwanted and unloved. His emotional propensity, separation from his new wife and daughter, along with the daily threat of dying in war set Dad up for an emotional tornado like no other. Drinking alcohol and smoking dope were common for many of the troops in Vietnam, Dad told me. It wasn't like they were going to sit around and sing Kumbaya or share their feelings with a counselor in the field of battle. PTSD wasn't even a thing yet, but self-medication was and so my Dad's epic battle with alcohol, anger and violence began.

Dad served eight years in the Marines total. In fact, Jimmy was born in Iwakuni, Japan just off the mainland of Okinawa. Both Terri and Jimmy spoke as much Japanese as they did English when they left Japan. Later, I was born at the Naval Hospital on Camp Pendleton near Oceanside, California in July 1973.

While Vietnam was a terrible time in Dad's life, he did like some aspects of the military life. It was a steady, solid paycheck and career. He had decided that he was in it for the long haul. The problem was, the Marine Corps decided he wasn't.

Dad said that he was always a bit heavy for his height. When Vietnam was starting and they needed bodies, being overweight didn't seem to matter to the Marine Corps. However, since Vietnam was now officially over in January 1973, the United States was looking to scale back its military. Dad was terminated from his military career due to his weight. While this didn't seem to be a huge deal at the time, it left a bad taste in Dad's mouth about the Marine Corps and the government. But this sting was softened at the time by the fact that there was still hope of another financially stable career on the horizon.

After Dad was excommunicated by Uncle Sam from his military career, we moved back to Griffith, Indiana where there was promise of a financially lucrative career in the steel mills. In a day and time that cars and many products were still made out of heavy steel, the steel mills were booming with business. Dad got a steady job and made solid money for a couple of years. A year after starting, they were even able to buy their first house and we moved again to nearby Hobart Township.

However, technology was changing and steel was not being used as commonly anymore. This, coupled with the OPEC oil embargo and the Iranian revolution made for very inconsistent employment opportunities in the industry. The steel mills began laying people off for periods of time. Men would work the line for a few weeks or months and then be laid off for a few weeks or months. This continued for nearly a year before Dad gave up on the promise of it working out long term. Though we had already moved three times at this point in my four year old life, this is when our moving really began.

From October 1977 to January 1980, we moved twenty-eight distinctive times. When I say that we moved twenty-eight times, I don't mean from a house on one side of town to another across town. We moved from state to state to state. We started by leaving our house in Hobart Township and headed out west to Castle Rock, Colorado where we lived for a couple of months. However, our journey during these couple of years took us back east to Illinois, then Georgia, then back to Colorado, then to Wyoming, then back to Illinois, then back to Indiana, then up to Wisconsin, then out to Montana, then down to Florida, then back up to Indiana, then back to Montana, then back to Colorado, then back to Indiana, then back to Wisconsin, then out to Kansas, then down to Oklahoma, and further yet down to Taylor, Texas.

This is no exaggeration and sometimes during these years we had several moves within a state before leaving for another. As the family came together recently over Christmas, we found it difficult to remember how the moves fit and exactly what month and what order the moves came in, but one thing was clear. We moved cross country, back cross country, and back cross country multiple times. We took everything we owned with us each time. If it didn't go with us, we no longer owned it.

Dad would move from manual labor job to manual labor job. He would leave problem upon problem behind. Some of our moves were precipitated by a DUI, some by being reported to children's services and others by a fight or an argument with a boss. Dad had a way with words and would often bum his way across the country by stopping at churches and talking pastors into providing lunch or dinner or gas money or even a hotel overnight. We would pull into town and buy a newspaper. We used the newspaper to look for jobs and cheap places to live. When he called someone about a place to live, he would find a way to talk them out of having to pay a deposit to move in. If we weren't there long, we didn't even have to pay the first month's rent, and utilities were often left unpaid when we left.

In 1979, we lived in a house in the country near Medora, Indiana that did not have a working bathroom. We used the wooden outhouse about thirty feet from the house as our toilet, which sucked since we lived there in January. The house didn't even have running water. We used a hand pump in the kitchen and heated water on the stove. We also used a cattle trough warmer (normally used to keep cow troughs from freezing in the winter) in an old-fashioned claw tub to take baths. We shared bath water of course, for efficiency's sake. We heated the house with a wood stove. We retrieved slabs for free from the saw mill and cut them to fit until our arms fell off.

Ironically, at this house, we also owned a pony that was given to us. The pony just ate the grass in the field next to the house so it's not like we had to do anything to take care of it. When we left that house in less than a month to move on to Morocco, Indiana, we just left the pony tied up outside.

As Spring turned to Summer In Morocco, we spent several months running around like the kids that we were. We rode our bikes all around town. We were free to come and go in this much simpler and safer time in our country. Ironically, I also learned the word "rape" as my brother's friends held me down in the grass and forced me to yell it while running and laughing afterwards. My parents both worked and we had the house to ourselves often. Somehow, we were able to have a pool table and played often. However, we were not allowed to play when Mom and Dad weren't home because Dad was a stickler on taking good care of it.

One summer day, my siblings and I were all home alone. Terri had partially finished cutting my hair. I needed it cut and she said she could do it, so we decided to give it a try. She was about half way done when we heard a loud noise in the front room. Terri's boyfriend had removed the two pieces of plywood and table cloth that covered the pool table and allowed us to also use it as a dining room table. Terri, her boyfriend and I played pool for a while. We had been playing for about twenty minutes when Jimmy called out to us. Terri's boyfriend literally climbed on top of the table and ran across it to the doorway. We were flabbergasted and bewildered. We were so glad Dad wasn't there to see it.

"Come on, get out here!" my brother yelled to us. Jimmy and his friends had some fireworks that they wanted to launch. "Check this out!" my brother pointed to a beercan across the driveway as we exited the side door of the house. Suddenly, the beercan rose about six inches from the ground and a large hole exploded from the side. I was startled, but thought that it was pretty cool. Jimmy and his friends started laughing.

"We got more back by the garage! Let's go!" Jimmy said excitedly. We walked up the driveway to the garage located at the back corner of the house. My parent's Ford Galaxie 500 was parked in the driveway in front of the garage on the level spot. The rest of the driveway was on a bit of a hill.

"This is the perfect place to shoot these off," Jimmy's friend said referring to the level spot of the driveway.

"You better not shoot those off near Mom and Dad's car!" Terri warned them.

"Well, move it then!" he shot back.

"We can't move the car!" Terri exclaimed. "We don't have a license."

"Don't be such a wuss!" he said. "I can move it! I know how," he pleaded.

"No way!" Terri responded. "*I'll* move it. You guys will mess something up!" Terri climbed into the driver's side seat of the car and found the keys in the ignition. We assumed they were just sitting there waiting for us to use them. *People don't just leave keys in the ignition for nothing, right?* I jumped in the passenger seat and grabbed at the lap belt like we were going on a Sunday afternoon cruise.

"Where we going?" I laughed.

"We are just moving the car down the driveway," Terri explained. "We are not going anywhere," she warned me. I didn't care. It sure seemed like a fun thing to do anyway. Terri turned the key in the ignition, but it just hiccuped a couple of times.

"What's wrong?" I asked.

"I don't know. That's all I thought there was to it," Terri said, confused about the process. The driver's side door flung open and Jimmy stood there.

"You have to press on the gas stupid! Move over, let me do it," he said.

"No way!" Terri said. "I am not getting in trouble for you guys screwing something up!"

"Well, then press on the gas stupid," he explained. Terri turned the ignition again and then reached down and pressed the brake pedal as hard as she could and turned the keys again. The car hiccuped again, but wouldn't start.

"THE GAS! YOU IGNORAMUS!" Jimmy yelled, annoyed at Terri's lack of driving skills. "The pedal on the right!"

"Oh," she said. Terri pressed on the right pedal and turned the key again and the car, hiccuped again, but then suddenly roared to life as she pumped it again. The power in that car was incredible. It sounded as if you could race through the back of the garage, the yard and it would lurch onto the racetrack at any moment. It was kind of scary, particularly with Terri behind the wheel. Terri grabbed at the lever by the steering wheel and pulled it over to the right, but it wouldn't move. She kept yanking at it to no avail.

"You are going to break it!" Jimmy said. "You have to press on the brake for it to move." Jimmy always seemed to know things that we didn't, especially when it came to cars, guns, bikes, the military, and well, just about everything. Terri pressed on the brake, leaning her short body down below the steering wheel to reach it. She then pulled the lever over until the triangle on the steering column pointed to the R letter. The car lurched backward, but didn't go anywhere with Terri's foot still pressing on the brake pedal. However, it was enough for the car door to bump Jimmy and knock him backward a couple of feet.

"What the h*ll?!!" Jimmy yelled.

"Well, get out of the way and close the door," she responded. Jimmy moved out of the way and slammed the door shut. I thought it was going to smack Terri in the face, except that it stopped as it reached its closed resting place. Terri released her foot from the brake pedal and the car slowly rolled backward. She let it go for another twenty or thirty feet and then pressed on the brake again. The car had moved backward at an angle instead of moving straight since Terri was pretty clueless about what she was doing. Short, little twelve year old girls don't get a lot of driving experience. Luckily, she had stopped the car prior to it continuing in that direction since there was a large tree directly behind the car now as it was angled off of the driveway.

"It's fine. We'll put it back." she said as she smiled at me. I smiled back happily, as I enjoyed our little trip down the driveway. We both got out and walked back up to where the boys were with the fireworks.

"Whattya got?" I asked. Jimmy's buddy showed us his Black Cat firecrackers, Magic Black Snake pellets, Roman Candles, Smoke Bombs, and a couple of M-80s. "Whoah!" I exclaimed. Fireworks were a boy's best friend. We spent the next couple of hours shooting them off and periodically throwing a smoke bomb or single firecracker at my sister. The Roman Candle was my favorite and we shot them up from the level patio spot.

The previous year we lived in Jacksonville, Florida near my aunt. We had been at her house shooting fireworks for New Year's Eve. I was holding a Roman Candle to shoot off when suddenly, one of them got stuck and the Roman Candle blew up in my hand. *Fireworks were always fun and well worth the risk*, I thought.

We lit the Magic Snake pellets and watched the snake grow magically before our eyes. We found inanimate objects to blow up as well as the occasional toad, to see if we could separate their body parts. The only thing better than throwing a sizzling smoke bomb at my sister was smelling the scent of burning sulfur. It was all so fun! Until my parents came home.

This was another one of those moments where glory turned into a nightmare. We had so much fun shooting off fireworks, playing pool, driving the car down the driveway and running around that we lost track of time and suddenly our parents were home.

"What the hell happened to the car?!" my dad yelled as he entered the side door of the house from the driveway. Terri and I had been in the living room watching TV and we sprinted to the side window by the driveway. We looked out and saw the Galaxie 500 leaning into the large tree that was next to the driveway. It appeared to have rolled the rest of the way into the tree.

"We don't know!" Terri claimed. "We never touched it." Mom had entered behind Dad with Shelby who was almost a year old at this time. Mom's eyes lit up when she saw me. At first, I was confused by her look. But, then I remembered the haircut Terri gave me. Or rather half a haircut, as it turned out. Dad entered fully into the front room and his eyes darted directly to the pool table that had been left undone, balls strewn across the tabletop. The covering plywood pieces were still against the wall and the tablecloth that had been covering them was strewn in a heap on the floor. I wanted to open my mouth to respond with some made up excuse when my dad noticed the footprints on the tabletop. The rest of that day was a blur. There was a lot of crying and spankings and yelling.

Terri ran away that evening, but the cops later brought her home. I don't know the conversations that took place, but we ended up moving the next day to Portage, Indiana. Portage was the same town that my mom would live in two years later after she left Dad.

While we had a lot of moves across the country, we often found ourselves in some of the same places, again and again. Like the time that we moved from Huntingbird, Indiana out west into Nevada, Montana, and New Mexico living in each of those places for at least a week but winding up in Loogootee, Indiana a few months later, just thirty miles from Huntingbird.

Chapter 9

The Summer Move (1982)

Walking down the hallway of my latest school gave me both a familiar feeling that all schools are pretty similar and an unfamiliar feeling that I was still learning my way around. Yet, I was also filled with happiness and a sense of freedom because summer had arrived. We were just a few days from the end of the school year and I knew that meant days of riding bikes, finding half-dead snakes and pools of tadpoles. Since we had just moved here to Huntingbird not that long ago, we probably weren't moving soon so I had a lot to look forward to for the summer. I remember walking down that hallway of school two days before my last day of third grade thinking, *wouldn't that*

be crazy to start at the same school in the fall that I finished in the spring?! I laughed to myself.

Riiinnnggg!!! The bell in the hallway shrilled. I had been coming back from the restroom, but that bell meant it was time for the school day to end so I quickly adjusted my route and headed to the bus. The hallways filled up and overflowed with kids heading home. As I headed to the bus, I realized that I had left several personal items in the classroom and in my cubby to take home. *Oh well,* I thought. *I'll just get them tomorrow.* I quickly continued to my bus.

Excitement filled the warm air outside as birds chirped and the sun shone brightly. Summer had definitely arrived! I hopped on the bus with an extra bit of excitement and found a seat next to a window where I could peer out as we headed home. Voices were loud and excited and we were all filled with joy and anticipation. The bus pulled out after the last kid jumped on and the light glistened through the windows as we passed by the shadows of the trees to our home destinations. My mind was filled with wonder as I looked forward to running around after school that afternoon.

One by one the bus stopped and dropped off my fellow classmates and students. Finally, about two-thirds of the way through the bus route, the bus pulled to a stop and it was time for me to finally arrive home. We pulled into the front of the rackety old house out in the country and I quickly exited the bus. I had pretty much kept to myself on the bus, hoping some bigger kid wouldn't pick on me. I had made it through another day and now was free as I stepped off the bottom step of the bus. The sun continued to shine brightly on my face and I was ready to run to grab my bicycle when I noticed our car in front of the house. It was a 1967 four-door olive green Chevy Impala. By today's standards, the car was huge.

Suddenly, my heart sank as I noticed a set of box springs and a mattress on top of the car. There was the beginning of the first row of boxes on top of the mattress. I knew what that meant. *It was time to move on.* I had no idea. So much for gathering my personal belongings the next day. So much for entering those hallways in the fall. So much for being able to just run and play this summer. *Who knew where we would end up? Who knew how long it would take to arrive?*

"Shawn!" my dad called. "Hey buddy, guess what?! Summer starts a few days early!" he said excitedly. "We're headed out west! We're going to the mountains!" Most kids might have imagined fun times camping or hiking excursions that might lay ahead of them. Except, I knew we weren't headed out on vacation. I knew campfires weren't in our future. We were loading up everything we could carry on our car and moving our entire belongings to the next destination, wherever that was going to be.

"Really?" I said, trying to hide my disappointment. It wasn't so much *the move* that disappointed me as it was the *not knowing*. I had my summer of freedom planned. *So much for plans with my family*, I thought. It seemed we would *never settle down.*

"Yep! Do you remember Colorado?" he asked me.

"Uh, yeah, sure. I think," I mumbled trying to remember which stop that was. Mountains came into my mind, but no particular mountains. I couldn't really remember anything specific, just the fact that we had lived in Colorado for a few months and there had been mountains at some point in our travels. I also remembered that there wasn't much grass or many trees, not the kind of trees with big trunks and big leaves anyway. I loved the grass in Indiana. It was plush and it was comfy enough to walk on with your bare feet or to lay on and read a book. The big oak and maple trees in Indiana were also a lush green and full of life. In contrast, the trees in Colorado were dry and filled with pine needles that poked and prodded your feet when you ran around without shoes.

I quickly scurried into the house and saw that Jimmy and Terri were already home and helping to pack up and load the car. I ran to my room and began to scan it to see what had already been packed and what I wanted to make sure made it in a box. I found my stack of baseball cards that included my Pete Rose special that all of the other kids tried to trade me for. That card was worth a quarter all by itself! They were crazy if they thought I was going to trade it. It was my prized possession. I also poked my head into my closet and found my stack of Marvel comic books that were laying there. Amazing stories of superpowers and real people with real issues in real cities piled upon each other.

That was the difference between Marvel and DC comics. I loved Marvel so much better! I never read or collected DC comics because the characters in their books just weren't very real. DC characters were old school, more descriptive of an era gone by. DC personas were "perfect" superhero people with alter egos that were used to hide their real identity. Marvel comic superheroes, on the other hand, were real people that happened to have superpowers. Marvel heroes would hide their real identity by donning costumes. DC comic stories were set in Metropolis and Gotham City; locations that didn't really exist and we could never visit. I didn't relate. Marvel's stories however, were set in Chicago and New York and Los Angeles. Periodically, Marvel superheroes interacted with real people such as the president or some other famous person.

My collection primarily consisted of Daredevil, Wolverine, The Uncanny X-men, and the earth's mightiest heroes; the Avengers! Jimmy collected GI Joe, Ghost Rider and Iron Man. It seemed like his choices were definitely more reminiscent of an older reader who loved guns more than the heroes themselves! I gathered up my most prized possessions and found an empty box. I put them in carefully, and organized them so they wouldn't get smashed or fall out of the box. I opened my dresser drawers and began piling my clothes into the box, being careful to pack so that my valuables would not be damaged. I closed up the box by setting the lid of the banana box on top of the piled belongings. I was careful to keep a large pillow in the center to cover the opening in the center of the box.

Even at my young age of eight, almost nine years old, I knew how to pack efficiently and effectively. I had learned how to pack and load as much as how to brush my teeth or tie my shoes. It was an art form and we perfected it. We did it *and* we did it quickly.

"Let's get going!" my dad yelled. "We've got to head out before it gets too dark." I knew we had several hours left, but those hours would fly by as we packed. We carried all of our belongings outside and loaded them on and in the car as quickly as we could. I knew I wasn't going to have a chance to tell my friend, Bryan, goodbye.

Bryan was pretty much the only kid that had befriended me in Huntingbird. I typically stayed pretty quiet and shy. I kept to myself not knowing how long we would be somewhere, and observed the culture, trying to fit in at first. I never quite felt like the fitting in part ever happened though, since we were usually moving on to our next location about the time that might start.

We finally got loaded up and as the sun was setting, we tied off the final ropes for secure traveling. The load on top of the car was all tied together, holding the boxes in on one level. There were three or four ropes with each layer of boxes. Boxes went up on top of the box springs and mattress that provided the foundation. Ropes traveled across the car from the driver's side to the passenger side, up over the top of the load on top and back around through the open window on the other side. We pulled the ropes tightly together and tied them in a knot securing the load to the roof. We did this three times; once in the front as far forward as we could slide it, once in the middle just behind the driver's door, and then again at the opening of the back door and window. Ropes were also tied front to back, traveling from the front bumper area up over the load on top and then down on the backside to the rear bumper tying it off where the rear bumper met the frame.

Off we went into the night, traveling along the backroads. Traveling the backroads kept us from drawing too much attention from the police on the highway. That was the last thing my dad wanted. We laid down on top of all the stuff in the backseat that created a bed-like structure for us kids. It was actually pretty comfortable. We were able to lay down and our legs extended into the rear window deck. While it was comfortable, we were also way too close to each other and had no place to escape our siblings. We quickly fell asleep that night as the sun set and Dad was driving quietly into the night. As much as he loved music, he rarely listened to it as we traveled.

We awoke the next morning laying on blankets in the grass. When I woke up and looked around, I noticed that we had taken our blankets out into the grass at a rest stop and fallen asleep. This was my first, and only family "camping experience." Jimmy was waking up at the same time. We were both a bit foggy.

"Where are we at?" I asked Jimmy.

"We're camping!" he answered sarcastically.

"What?" I asked, not getting it.

"This is how we camp. No tent. No sleeping bags. Grab your blanket and your pillow. We're camping!" he repeated. I just shook my head, not remembering when we arrived or got out of the car. Mom and Dad laid under their own blanket just a few feet away, still sleeping. Apparently, when Dad got tired of driving, we stopped and got out of the car with our blankets and went to sleep. I guess I never woke up in the whole process because I couldn't recall anything from the night before.

Everyone else started to stir as the rest stop had a few cars pull in and out of the parking lot. Shelby, who was now almost four years old was sleeping close to Mom and Dad on Mom's side. Shannon was now almost two years old and was sleeping with Jimmy and I. We all slowly got up, went to the bathroom and took our sleeping gear back to the car without saying much. Mom and Dad awoke while we were in the restroom and now were in the car. Mom gave us some doughnuts from a grocery bag on the front floor on the passenger side.

"Who wants some milk?" my dad asked as he pulled a gallon of milk out of the cooler filled with half-melted ice. Jimmy and I shot our hands up. I couldn't imagine eating doughnuts without drinking milk. That would be a travesty! We all ate up, took some fresh clothes back into the restrooms and changed. "Don't forget to wash under your armpits," Dad reminded us. We were given a bar of soap, a washcloth and expected to *shower up* in the restroom. All things considered, Dad was a stickler on staying clean. He insisted we stay bathed and clean no matter our living conditions. We all washed up, changed clothes and got back on the road again.

Periodically, we pulled into a small town on a back road and stopped at a church that had a parsonage next door. That's how you knew the pastor would be around. He lived right next to his work.

Dad exited the vehicle and walked right up to the house or the church office, if they had one. We watched him knock on the door. Pretty soon after, the door opened, greetings were exchanged and then Dad went inside. After a good fifteen or twenty minutes, Dad and the pastor emerged from the house and walked back to the vehicle. My mom smiled and waved. I'm sure we looked as homely as we could and hoped for some nice reward from the pastor.

"How far are you all going?" I heard the pastor ask my dad.

"Just up the road a good thirty miles to Nashville," my dad explained, meaning Nashville, Illinois. "I've got a job waiting for me there. We're almost there and just need this little bit to get us the last bit of the way there. Lunch would be great too, if you got any food."

Dad used this tactic every time. *Don't tell them how far you are going or let them think you are wandering aimlessly.* He told them that we were almost there and that he planned to work for his money very soon. They believed him and trusted that he was an honest, hard working man trying to take care of his family and just ran out of money before they arrived at their new destination. Typically, it worked, as it did that day.

I saw the pastor talking to Dad and pointing. Next thing I knew, Dad got in the car and said, "He's gonna fill us up! Lunch is on him at this place called Frankies. Don't any of you kids say a word about where we are going," Dad warned us. Dad pulled out and followed the pastor who led us in his car. We pulled into the gas station, filled up and then had lunch at Frankies on the pastor's bill. Later that day, I noticed Dad had plenty of cash in his trucker's style wallet that was hanging from his belt loop and sticking out of his back pocket.

"How come we stopped at that church if you have money Dad?" I asked hoping that I wouldn't get my block knocked off. Dad just laughed.

"That's why I have cash! Because these idiots will keep taking care of us. Just watch and learn son," he explained, proud of himself. We left out of town after lunch and this experience repeated itself time after time, town after town, church after church. Thankfully, many times a church put us up for the night in a motel while we were traveling because I don't remember ever sleeping in the grass at a road stop again after that first night. Eventually, within a week or two we ended up in Hawthorne, Nevada. Upon arriving in Hawthorne, Dad found us a house to rent. He was able to talk the owner out of a deposit and told him we would pay it with our first month's rent at the end of the month.

We weren't there long. Just a week or two after Dad got in an argument at work. He got in a fist fight with his boss after going to work half-drunk, half-hung over from the night before. We were quickly back on the road again, next arriving in Missoula, Montana. Dad went to some agency when we arrived, trying to find work and a place to stay. They put us up in an old apartment building that was used as a weekly motel for needy housing. Dad looked for work there, but couldn't find it and within three weeks, we were back on the road again. My only memories there were the motel itself and having someone from the newspaper take our picture in front of the car as we told our sob story. It didn't help enough to find a decent job though and we were back on the road again.

As we were traveling through Utah into Arizona, I remember being amazed at the scenery in the area. Large, red rocks were everywhere and it was so beautiful, but it was also extremely hot, as we traveled through southern Utah in that Impala with no air conditioner and stuffed away in the back of the car. The sun baked our feet in the back window. We were sweating and exhausted without ever moving. Looking back at my feet in the back window, I noticed a large truck with a trailer. The truck was flashing its lights and swerving a little bit. All of the sudden, we all heard honking and the truck passed us by. As it passed by on the driver's side, the lady in the passenger seat of the truck was waving her arms wildly.

The truck continued to pass us by and pulled into our lane directly in front of us. The truck was very nice and it was pulling a lengthy RV trailer. Suddenly, the RV trailer's brake lights lit up as the truck was slowing down pretty significantly, directly in front of us without even pulling over. Dad slowed the car and began to wonder what the heck was going on.

"Candy, check out the load. Do you think we lost something?" Dad asked, thinking maybe something had fallen off the car. Mom, put her head out the window as the car continued to slow down.

"I don't know," she said. "I don't see anything."

The truck came to a stop and finally pulled off to the side. Dad decided to go ahead and pull over behind him as he saw the guy trying to wave him to the side of the road while pulling his truck over. After we came to a stop, the man exited his truck and walked back to our car.

"Howdy!" the happy, excited driver greeted us. He looked around and saw the sweltering conditions we were experiencing in the car. "Can I talk to you a moment, sir?" he asked my dad.

"Sure?" my dad answered confused.

"Over here," he explained motioning toward his RV trailer side that was away from the highway. My dad got out and followed him. We all hoped we hadn't lost something significant off the top. I was so afraid that my bike was long gone. Dad and him talked for a few minutes. We could all see them talking, but couldn't hear a word they said. Then, the man pulled his wallet out of his pocket and gave Dad some cash. He embraced my dad, giving him a hug, waved to us with a big smile and returned to his vehicle. The truck and RV trailer slowly returned to the highway and pulled away. Dad returned to the driver's seat with a big smile on his face.

"What was that all about?" Mom asked. We all looked forward, anticipating the story with deep interest.

"That guy just gave me two hundred dollars!" Dad exclaimed.

"What?! What for?" Mom asked.

"He didn't really say. Just said we looked like we needed it more than him," he laughed. We all laughed. I'm sure we did need it more than him. "Oh, and he said, 'God bless you!'"

We stopped in Tucson, Arizona for a few weeks that summer. We lived in a trailer park and in a trailer that had one window air conditioner. We were only allowed to use the air conditioner at night due to some story about it breaking down or not being useful enough. Every day that summer the temperature was about a hundred and four degrees. It seemed almost every day about two o'clock in the afternoon, the wind would pick up and start blowing really hard for about fifteen minutes and then it would rain down heavily for about another ten or fifteen minutes. Afterwards, the sun would come out and everything would return to its normal sweltering heat. We weren't there long before we hit the road again. I'm betting that summer in Nevada, Utah and Arizona made my dad hate the heat because he always talked about hating the heat as a kid.

After we left Arizona, we went through New Mexico, Texas, Oklahoma, Missouri, Illinois and eventually, back into Indiana. Shortly after we left, we stopped at a gas station along the way and picked up a stray kitten. It was so cute and I couldn't believe Dad let us keep it. But it wasn't long before we all started breaking out with ringworm and we knew the culprit was this stray cat. We let the cat go stray, but couldn't shake the ringworm.

Around the end of August, we arrived in Washington, Indiana just thirty-two miles from Huntingbird where we had left at the end of the school year. We had spent an entire summer on the road, unloading the car a few times, but quickly reloading and back on the road again. We received help after help after help while probably not paying any of our bills at our stops. Dad found time and money for his alcohol though. He worked a few times, though not for long each time.

We pulled into Washington after being on the road for a couple of days. Dad stopped at a church and disappeared inside the office attached to the building. About an hour later, he returned with some papers in his hand, thanking the gentleman. Dad returned to the vehicle, sat down and sighed.

"What's going on?" Mom asked.

"I can't believe it," he said. "This guy is putting us up in a motel downtown for two weeks, getting us some food and some help for the kids' ringworm." We all sighed with relief. We were tired of being in that vehicle and we were miserable from scratching ourselves constantly. We went to the hotel, took showers, and changed clothes. We went to bed, glad to finally be settling down again. We hoped.

The next morning, I was excited about the prospect of getting to ride my bicycle. Jimmy and I went downstairs to get our bikes off the car. Jimmy had to clean the spark plugs in the car as part of our very limited maintenance routine. I climbed up on the stacked mess to get our bikes down after cutting the rope that was securing them to the top. About that time, a newspaper reporter stopped by and began asking us questions. He took our picture as we cut our bikes down and then followed us up to our hotel room. They took our picture again in the hotel room and Dad gave him his best sob story. The next day, our pictures were in the paper again and Dad got a job offer the following day. Finally, we thought we were able to settle down again. We enrolled in school there that fall to start the school year, just thirty two miles from where we left at the end of the previous school year.

At this point in my story, nothing should be surprising. However, we ended up living in Loogootee, Indiana for a third stint just over a year later. But this time, we would live there without our parents.

Chapter 10

Loogootee Pt 3 (1982-1983)

We were in Washington, Indiana for about two weeks. Dad didn't like his job and decided to move on. The next eighteen months were a blur. Even as the family that lived it, none of us can recall exactly where we were and when during this time span. However, in late September 1982, we were on our way again. We arrived back in Loogootee for a third time, fully loaded down in typical fashion.

Actually, just prior to arriving in Loogootee, we stopped at a restaurant to get something to eat for lunch. We parked out front by the road and walked inside to eat. About halfway through our meal, a police officer walked into the restaurant and spoke to the manager. We all had grown leary of the police.

Whenever they were around, we were likely to be in trouble and we feared their involvement in our lives. We all kept eating quietly with our heads down hoping the cop would not see us. The manager spoke to the police officer for a couple of minutes and then pointed to our table. My dad pretended not to notice, but I knew something was wrong.

The police officer walked over to our table.

"Is that your car out there?" the policeman asked, pointing out the window to our car.

"Yes, sir. Is there a problem?" my dad asked politely. My dad knew his long hair, beard and moustache were likely to draw negative attention from the police, so he did his best to be respectful. He felt as if he had been treated poorly by cops because of his hippy-like appearance ever since he returned from Vietnam and was excommunicated from the Marine Corps.

"You're gonna have to move your car," he explained.

"What? What do you mean? Why?" my dad asked quizzically.

"That's why," he stated, pointing out the window to our car. We all looked out the window toward our overloaded car. Traffic on the street was crawling in both directions as people looked out their windows and gawked at our vehicle. It was as if an accident had happened and no one could take their eyes off the entertainment of the day. "Your vehicle is causing a distraction. I'm gonna need you to move it around back where people can't see it."

We all wanted to laugh immediately. It *was* a distraction. But, we maintained our cool and Dad responded, "Oh. Of course, right away officer."

The officer tipped his hat and said, "Have a nice day." Dad got up and went out the door to move the car. As soon as both the officer and my dad were outside, we busted up laughing.

"Well that was a new one," Jimmy said. We all shook our heads, finished our meal and left. We went around back, got in the car and headed off to our destination.

To this day, I don't know if Loogootee for a third time was our intention or not. We definitely wanted to visit my sister Terri who lived in a foster home just outside of Loogootee. Mom and Dad may have had something up their sleeve to "rescue her" from her foster family and take off again. I don't remember it, but I'm told we stopped first at Terri's foster home and visited with her and her foster family for only a few minutes before they asked us to leave. I imagine Dad got in an argument with her foster mom.

We arrived in Loogootee about mid-afternoon and stopped at the local Huck's gas station/mini-mart which had been recently built since the last time we had lived there. Dad went inside to get a newspaper to read the classified ads. He needed to see if he could find work and a place to live. We sat out in the car waiting.

"Mom can we get a slushie?" I asked. We had eaten not that long ago, but I always had room for a *Huck's* slushie!

"I don't think so. We don't have much money right now and we need to find a place to live first," Mom explained.

"Please!!" I pleaded. "They are only ten cents!" I said as I pointed out the car window to the advertisement on the window of *Huck's*. The advertisement was a poster showing the ten different flavors you could create. About that time, a police officer rolled up behind us and parked nearby. We all cringed, fearing what they might say about our car this time. Two policemen exited the car and looked in our direction. About that time, my dad walked out of *Huck's* with a newspaper in his hand. The policemen had turned around and he caught their eye. They followed him with their eyes as he walked toward our vehicle hoping to keep a low profile. As my dad approached our vehicle, the policemen followed, this time with their feet.

My dad became aware of their approach and turned toward them.

"Can I help you?" Dad asked.

"Is this your vehicle?" one of them asked.

"Yes, sir. Is there a problem?" he answered politely and respectfully.

"We need to speak with you a moment. Can you follow us?" the same policeman replied. They motioned in the direction of their car and Dad followed. They spoke for what seemed like an eternity, but was probably only about five minutes. Afterwards, they all walked back toward our vehicle. Mom had rolled the window down to try and hear what was going on. We were all so silent you could hear a pin drop. As they approached the vehicle, Dad came around to the driver's side with one cop, and the other approached the passenger side where I was sitting next to my mom in the front seat, while Jimmy, Shelby and Shannon were all laying down in the back.

"Good afternoon, ma'am." the policeman greeted. "How are you kids doing?" he continued.

"Fine." Most of us replied in unison. The officer bent down and looked into the vehicle to assess the situation.

"I'm gonna have to ask you all to step out of the car, please," he explained. We all got out of the car, wondering what we had done. I opened the passenger door and jumped out first. Mom followed. Jimmy rolled into the front seat, reached back for Shelby and Shannon and helped them roll into the front seat so that they could exit the vehicle. Dad was standing on the driver's side talking to the other cop after grabbing his driver's licence from inside the vehicle.

"Ma'am, can we see the registration please?" the officer continued. Mom reached back in the car and opened the glove box, extracting the registration from within.

"Here you go," she said, still wondering what all of this was about. We all stood outside of the vehicle as if in a lineup, leaning against the passenger side of the car awaiting further instructions.

"Thank you," he said. "I'll be right back." About that time, the officer with my dad walked back around the car, apparently holding my dad's license and followed the other cop back to their car. Dad came around to our side of the car and stood by my mom.

"This is bullsh*t," he whispered to my mom. "We haven't done anything. I haven't been drinking. We haven't broken any laws."

"Jim, quiet!" she whispered back, "or they will find something." We waited again for what seemed like an eternity as they sat in their car with my dad's license, our registration and our future in their possession. About that time, the police officer on the driver's side got back out of his car and returned.

He approached my dad saying, "Mr. Conjeltun, I'm gonna have to ask you to come back with me." He motioned back toward his police car. My dad followed and we all stayed waiting on the side of the car. The other policeman exited the vehicle and walked toward us again.

As he approached, he explained, "Ma'am, you and your kids will have to come with us."

"What? Why? What is going on? We haven't done anything," my mom pleaded.

"Ma'am, there has been a report about your kids living in these deplorable conditions," he explained motioning to our vehicle. We found out later that my sister's foster mom had called the police on us.

"We are moving!" she pleaded. "We just arrived. We are looking for a home and work. That's why my husband went inside; to get a paper to help us find them!" she said with a quiver in her voice almost crying.

"I understand, ma'am. But this is not acceptable. These children need something better *right now*." About that time, another police car pulled up. He directed us four kids into the back of this new cruiser and directed my mom into the passenger's seat. As we entered the car, we sat behind the grid of metal between the front of the car and the backseat. I looked out the window and saw the other cop directing my dad into the back of the first police cruiser.

The next thing I remember, we were in some strange building with social services and they were discussing how they could not find a home for four kids at a time. We gave Mom hugs and kisses as they whisked us away from her. She was in tears, feeling hopeless and miserable. She didn't know what was going to happen. Terri was already in a foster home here in Loogootee and now they had taken her other four kids.

We were directed into the back of a government vehicle. A nice lady drove us out of Loogootee, about eight miles over to the next town, Shoals. Just outside of town, we pulled up to a nice house on the edge of a hill.

"We're here," she announced. None of us really knew what that meant. "Let's go," she said and got out of the driver's seat. Jimmy, sitting behind the driver's seat, opened the door and got out, looking back at us in expectation of us following him. Shelby and I got out and we helped Shannon get out afterwards. He was now just three years old, having his birthday the previous month. "Follow me," she said and began walking up to the front door. She knocked on the door and awaited an answer. The door opened and a middle-aged lady with tight curls and large octagonal eyeglasses peered out.

She smiled and said, "Come on in!" and she opened the screen door. We all walked in the house not knowing what to expect. Two large friendly dogs approached us and began to sniff us to determine if we were friendly. Jimmy, loving dogs, quickly petted one and walked in confidently. I was a bit more sheepish and stayed back, hoping I wasn't getting dropped off at this location. We all entered fully into the house and walked into the living room.

"We've got room for two of them," the lady from this house said to our driver. "Who wants to stay?" she asked as she directed her attention to us. Jimmy was enthusiastically petting one of the dogs and looked up.

"I'll stay. Shannon can stay with me," he added matter of factly. I was relieved. This lady seemed weird and I did not want to live with these two dogs. Somehow, I knew this wasn't going to be just overnight. I gave a look of *"fine by me"* but didn't say anything as I continued to look sheepishly at the lady.

"Well, that was easy," she laughed and our driver escorted Shelby and I back out to the car. Shelby and I returned to the back seat of the car, not even saying bye to, or giving Jimmy and Shannon a hug. She drove us back to Loogootee and into what seemed to be a newer housing neighborhood. *Yes*, I thought, *at least we will get to stay in a nice house*. We pulled up to a single story, brick ranch style home and got out. The lady led us to the door and knocked. The door opened shortly after and a nice lady with a full brunette perm in her early forties answered the door.

Shelby and I lived there for a couple of months. I went to fifth grade in Loogootee, at the middle school across town from where the elementary school was that I previously attended during our second time in Loogootee. I made some friends down the street and I went over to their house often to play Frogger and sled down the hill in the snow. Shelby and I played a lot of Connect Four at our foster home where we lived with this family. They had two teenage kids who wanted nothing to do with us. Our foster mom had a ton of plants in her front room which was a little weird to us, but they were a nice family and took good care of us.

We were provided with all new clothes. I was able to get my first (and only) pair of *Underoos*, *Superman* style. We got new pants, new pajamas, new shoes and a new coat. They bought us school supplies and provided everything we needed, though I missed a few of my personal items like my comic books. I also missed my brothers who were living about ten miles away.

Our time in the foster home was fairly uneventful. I don't even remember interacting with Shelby too much. It was like we did our time in pleasant surroundings with pleasant people and moved on.

After a few months passed by, we found ourselves in a courtroom where the adults were talking about really important things. Jimmy and Shannon were there too. Mom and Dad were across the room and we were filled with conflicting emotions. All of us siblings really missed each other and Mom too. We even kind of missed Dad. We didn't know what was going on, but we wanted to go home, *wherever* that was. As it turned out, Mom and Dad had both found jobs and established a home for us to rejoin them. The court permitted us to return to our parents that day and we were relieved to be back together.

We exited the courthouse with our family and got back in our car which was now emptied of all of our belongings. Mom and Dad drove us to our new home in Loogootee that we thought we were going to live in.

When we arrived, Dad said, "Pack up. We're getting the h*ll out of here." Mom and Dad had found jobs, rented a house and made arrangements for us to live there. The court had released us back into their custody. Now, my dad was through with the way this town and government people had treated him and his family. They had already taken my sister permanently and threatened to keep us too. There was no way we were sticking around just to have someone try it again. We loaded up that next day, left town and left the state heading back out west to the great state of Wyoming.

While it may seem odd that we didn't express much emotion being taken from our parents, we really didn't know what to think. *Was it a good thing? Would we ever see them again? Would they take care of us better than our parents? Would we see Terri again soon?* We wondered all of these things, but the experience was way less emotional than being at home with Dad. We were slightly afraid, partly wondering if we were in trouble ourselves. We were confused and in shock a little bit, not really knowing how to react, just taking it all in and trying to understand what was happening. Due to moving constantly, we learned how to deal with just about any situation we found ourselves in. Looking back, our whole lives were about adjusting to new situations.

Chapter 11

Wandering (1975-1980)

It's difficult to describe how our moving took us cross country many times, especially in the early days. When I say we lived in twenty places in Colorado, we didn't always move from one place in Colorado to another. We often moved to Indiana, then Wisconsin, down to Kansas, up to Nebraska, over to Nevada, then back to a new place in Colorado. The best I can describe it is... we were *wandering*. The phrase, "Not all who wander are lost," comes to mind. We just **never settled** down in one place. I don't know that my dad had a heart for adventure as much as he left all of his problems behind every time, hoping to start anew and find a better life somewhere else. In all reality, he was lost. Very lost.

Back in April 1975, when I was only 21 months old, Dad had started his good job at the steel mills in northern Indiana. The job was good and the living was good. My parents bought their first house in Hobart Township. This was near where they grew up. They had just three kids at this time. Terri, my older sister of six years and Jimmy, my older brother of four years.

When the steel mill laid my dad off one too many times, our real wandering began. Dad saw the dangers in his line of work and watched a man literally fall into a vat of hot molten steel and disintegrate before his very eyes. The work was treacherous and challenging, but the money was good, until it wasn't. We lived there for two and a half years and then began wandering.

In October 1977, we moved out to Castle Rock, Colorado. We lived there for a couple of months and moved back east to Grant Park, Illinois. We lived there for a month and moved south to Savannah, Georgia where my aunt lived at the time. I only recently discovered that we even lived in Savannah. We weren't there but a few months though, when we moved back west to Colorado, landing in a trailer in Elizabeth, not too far from Castle Rock. That lasted less than a month as we found a house in nearby Elbert, still in Colorado at this point. In less than a month, we were off to Glenrock, Wyoming. Just a few weeks later, we were back on the road headed east to Paris, Illinois where my grandparents grew up and some of our extended family lived.

Another month later, we moved on to live in a house in the country near Horace, Illinois. We were able to get a dog there. We didn't often have a dog and when we did, we didn't have one very long. We had the unfortunate experience of naming our dog(s), Bacon. Not sure how or why they got that name, but the unfortunate part was every time we named our dog Bacon, they ended up getting hit by a car and killed.

This was true for the first time, living in the country near Horace. We weren't in Horace long though, when just a month later, we moved on to Donovan, Illinois where we lived in a very large house. Our route north continued from there when we moved back into Indiana and settled down in Fair Oaks where we rented a brand new duplex. Apparently, the nice new accommodations weren't enough to make us stick around. We lived there for two months before heading a little east over to Leiters Ford, Indiana in the early summer.

We lived in Leiters Ford for about three months, but I'm sure the reason we stuck around a little longer was, my mother was very pregnant. She gave birth to my younger sister, Shelby in a hospital in Winamac while we lived there. I was five years old that summer and once my mom recovered from having her, we moved again in August to Rhinelander, Wisconsin where I started Kindergarten. Having three kids in school didn't slow us down though and just two months later, we headed back out west, this time to Lavina, Montana.

I can only imagine how our school documents followed us or didn't follow us during our school transitions. I wonder if my parents even told them where we were previously. I'm sure if they did, they only told them about the previous stop. They must have kept our important documents like birth certificates and shot records readily available since they needed to constantly keep enrolling us in a new school. If they didn't have them, I'm sure it would have been a red flag for a school district to sick Children's Services on us. Amazingly, we only ended up in a foster home the one time in Loogootee (other than Terri & Jimmy running away in high school and finishing their high school careers in foster homes).

We moved into Lavina in October and out in December. We had an old coal furnace in that house that Jimmy had to keep stoked from the reserve in the basement. Terri played basketball in the eighth grade in Lavina, but not for long obviously.

I'm not sure if having to use a coal furnace or simply experiencing a winter in Montana had anything to do with it, but Terri had to quit the basketball team because we moved south to Jacksonville, Florida where one of my mom's sisters lived. Mom had the hope of getting a job at her work place. She worked for an insurance company and had hoped to start a solid career paying claims in the health insurance industry. Apparently, that never worked out there, most likely because we moved back to northern Indiana to live in Black Oak. My dad caught on at a steel mill again working for the Youngstown Steel Mill. Mom got her own job in or near Chicago and took the L-train to work everyday.

Our wandering didn't slow down or stop there though. Within a month, we moved back west to Roundup, Montana for the start of summer. One thing I loved about Roundup was the city pool. The city pool was free for the community. I learned how to swim that summer going to the pool with Terri and Jimmy. We went almost every day. The pool was full of community kids, but we had fun. The weather was nice and we were glad to be there. Of course, we weren't there long since we moved mid-summer to Bennett, Colorado.

In Bennett, both of my parents were gone from home one day. Terri and Jimmy were charged with watching Shelby and I. No problem. Except there was a fair going on that they wanted to go to and I was feeling sick. I wanted to go so bad too, but I was in constant fear of throwing up. Terri and Jimmy did what any responsible brother and sister would do. They (at twelve and ten respectively) took one-year-old Shelby with them to the fair where they spent the day engrossed in all the attractions; the rides, the games and the lights of the county fair while I (at six years of age) stayed home sick by myself. Unfortunately for them, Mom and Dad made it home before they did, but at least they had brought me a fair prize; my first wine glass.

For their enjoyment of the day (and ignoring me as their responsibility), Terri and Jimmy received their typical forty lashes of the belt. I felt bad for them and sad that I didn't get to go to the fair, but at least I got the wine glass. Of course, that didn't last long as I left it near the front door and it was knocked over and broken soon after. We weren't in Bennett for long either though because we moved back to Indiana, winding up in a house in the country near Medora.

Our house in Medora was unique for a couple of reasons. I remember moving in without any furniture. We may have had a few mattresses or the owner lent us a few. On top of that, the house didn't have any hot water. We heated water on the stove and used a horse trough milk warmer to heat our bath water, which of course, we shared. Also, the inside toilet didn't work. Yes, the inside toilet didn't work. We used the outhouse fifteen feet from the house as our daily toilet. If you've used a nice port-a-potty in the last twenty years, this is quite a different experience that I really don't want to describe.

The most unique experience of this house was that it came with a pony. This was the house with a pony. Yes, that's right. A pony. The owner of the house told us we could have the pony that lived on the property. It was tied up and I guess it ate the grass in the yard/field near the house because we never fed it.

We were only in Medora for about a month that winter, of course, but that house left a not-so-delightful memory etched in our brains forever. From Medora, we headed on to Morocco, Indiana where my story about the pool table, fireworks and the Galaxie 500 took place. We spent a few months in the summer in Morocco. We left Morocco and moved to Portage for the first time. Portage was where we lived a second time when Mom would later escape Dad after leaving him in a jail cell following his DUI in Loogootee. I started first grade in Portage.

From Portage, we moved to Tefft and then Demotte, Indiana staying for less than a month in both of those places. After Demotte, we moved back up to Wisconsin, stopping in Crandon where Jimmy shot Terri with his BB gun from over a block away. He thought it was an epic shot, but she was not as impressed. I'm sure she deserved it anyway. We quickly moved on to Laona, Wisconsin where my dad worked at the Louisiana Pacific paper mill. However, that was short lived since Dad got fired and arrested for smacking his foreman boss at work. We moved on quickly to Monico a few miles over, but that house was unlivable. It's hard to imagine how it was unlivable after living in Medora, but it must have been worse because we stayed there a very short time then moved on quickly to Ingalls, Kansas.

I'm not sure how intentional the location of each of our moves were. I don't see how we were doing anything but wandering. From time to time, something drew us to a particular location. Sometimes, it was a relative who lived nearby. Sometimes, the promise of a job. Sometimes, the promise of a new area that was yet to be discovered. Sometimes, Dad had a knowledge of the area based on previously living nearby. We wandered nonetheless.

From Ingalls, Kansas we moved on to Cheyenne, Oklahoma where Dad got another DUI so we moved on quickly to Taylor, Texas where I became a Pittsburgh Steelers fan when they played the Dallas Cowboys in the final of their four Super Bowls from their Steel Curtain defense era. Black and gold were pretty cool colors for a football team and everyone else where we lived was for the Cowboys. As the new kid in that town, I chose to root against everyone else's team and became a lifelong Steelers fan after they beat the Cowboys for their fourth Lombardi trophy in six years.

After school was out that year, Jimmy attended boy scout camp. When he returned home from the weeklong activity, no one came to the school to pick him up. He was able to get a ride from a friend, but when he arrived home he discovered the house was locked. He was able to jimmy open a window and get in, but then discovered that we had moved without him. Garbage was strewn throughout the house, but our belongings and family were gone. He went out to the front steps and cried only to have Mom and Dad show up a short time later. Apparently, they had the wrong time that the boy scouts would return from their trip and had simply moved across town this time due to the high number of cockroaches living with us. It wasn't long though before we moved again, this time to Grover, Colorado where Dad worked at a grain bin for a few weeks.

After those few weeks in Grover, we moved further west to Reno, Nevada where we lived in a hotel for about three weeks. I received my freedom in Reno by learning how to ride a bike. It was ugly learning without training wheels. I would get up on the banana seat and press off a wall, only to crash ten or fifteen feet down the sidewalk. I tried again and again, and eventually, I learned how to ride my bike and keep my balance without crashing. I loved riding my bike. It gave me that same sense of freedom, I'm sure, that the automobile gave my dad to wander.

From Reno, we moved on to Lovelock, Nevada where Dad picked up another DUI causing us to move quickly again; this time to Tucson, Arizona. In Tucson, we lived in that house trailer with no air conditioner. We had some box fans, but that was it. The day we moved out was one hundred and seventeen degrees. We couldn't get out quick enough.

From Tucson, we wandered back to Grover, Colorado. I guess my dad thought he would try his hand back at the grain bin. Maybe he was promised a job if he ever came back. Either way, Grover had much more reasonable summer weather. My brother, Shannon was born while we lived in Grover. He was even dedicated in a church in Grover by a female pastor, which looking back was odd because I rarely remember us going to church unless we needed a handout. I guess we needed a handout.

For some reason, the couple of blocks that consisted of the town Grover, held a special place in my dad's heart. This may have been another reason we went back for a second time. I started second grade and I went to a high school football game there. I ran around and played with a mini-football during the beginning of the National Anthem and was quickly scolded and reprimanded. This left an imprint in my mind that still causes me to scold and admonish kids, even today, if they disrespect the National Anthem or Pledge of Allegiance.

We bought a car called a Rambler while we lived in Grover and tried a new way to load up. We found a VERY LARGE box that took up the entire size of the roof of the car and filled it up with stuff from the house while it was on the car. We brought stuff from the house and tossed it into the box until it was full. It turned out that it was too heavy for the car and caused it to sag down pretty significantly in the rear. We made it a few hours to Ault, Colorado where we *tried* to settle down.

As the perennial new kid in school, I was always quiet. I typically kept to myself initially. I observed my surroundings and culture and then tried to fit in once I thought I understood it. We weren't in Ault long enough to try and fit in yet. I was still in my quiet, observation phase.

One day at school, I was feeling sick so I walked up to the front of the class where several students were in line at the teacher's desk waiting for her to look at their schoolwork. As I waited patiently, I began feeling like I was going to puke. I was afraid to jump the line or speak up for myself. Once my turn finally came, I stepped up to the teacher, but I was feeling so bad at that point my stomach began to lurch. The teacher could tell I wasn't feeling well and asked why I was acting like I had to throw up. When I went to answer her, my stomach erupted and I finally threw up all over her lap and desk. I was actually pretty glad we got to move from there quickly.

We moved from Ault, Colorado to Chrisman, Illinois, but only for a week. We were back on the road again. About a week later, we wandered into or rather near Loving, New Mexico. That old Rambler had enough of that big old box on top. While we were traveling along the two lane highway, in what seemed to be the middle of nowhere in the desert of New Mexico, the rear axle snapped. We ended up living in Loving, New Mexico near Carlsbad Caverns for a few weeks as Dad looked for a job, so that we could buy another car.

Work was hard to find there and eventually he gave up looking. We took everything we could fit in suitcases and/or handbags that we could carry. We walked out of town to the side of the highway in the New Mexican desert with all of our belongings and a cardboard sign that read: Loogootee, Indiana. Mom, Dad and all five kids at the time; Terri (13), Jimmy (11), me (7), Shelby (2), Shannon (one month) stood on the side of the road with our thumbs out. We were determined to hitchhike to Loogootee, Indiana. Once again, not sure how Loogootee became our intended destination, but this was how we *first* moved into Loogootee. That small town in southern Indiana wasn't a place anyone would choose out of nowhere. People don't even know how to pronounce it if they haven't been there before.

Now let me tell you, not many people have extra room for seven additional people while driving down the road. It was a good thing for us that this happened before our current laws of seatbelts and not riding in the bed of a pick-up truck. After what seemed like forever, a gentleman in a pickup truck stopped to give us a ride. Mom, Dad and Shannon sat up front with the driver. The rest of us jumped in the back with our luggage. Our adventure continued as we *wandered* (moved) without a vehicle and everything we could carry with us.

We made it as far as the panhandle of Texas when a kind couple picked us up in their truck. They gave us a ride into the next town where they lived and put us up in a hotel. The next morning they took us to their church and the pastor bought us bus tickets the rest of the way to Loogootee. We ended up getting off the bus in Illinois though, because Dad did not want people to get the wrong idea when we arrived in Loogootee. He was afraid they would think we had enough money to ride a bus. It's amazing to think about how we got from one place to the next at times.

Chapter 12

The Last Days of Jimmy (1983 - 1984)

After we left Loogootee for the third and final time, we ventured back west to Wyoming. We arrived first in Pine Bluffs. The topography of this area was very unique and one that we enjoyed as kids. The bluffs were beautiful in their own right and we saw them as an adventure each time we got a chance to explore the uncharted territory. Jimmy and I would hike up into the bluffs every chance we had.

"What are we gonna do?" I asked Jimmy, as we headed across the street and into the wilderness.

"We're going hunting!" he explained. We continued into the field covered with tall grass, which turned out to actually be hay. We trotted through the field with our guns. Jimmy had his pellet gun and I had my BB gun. We were going hunting.

"But, what are we going to hunt?" I asked, confused. We had tried to shoot birds from time to time, but never really had a chance to hunt anything else. I was excited for a chance to hunt something larger, but wondered how our little guns were going to allow us to do that.

"I guess we'll find out. Whatever we can get. Rabbits, prairie dogs, squirrels or whatever we have a chance at!" Jimmy said. I was pretty sure if we found a coyote or a mountain lion, we would be hunting those with our little guns too. Jimmy had all the confidence in the world that we could take on any challenge. He was the one I wanted by my side if *Red Dawn* ever happened for real. We were Matt and Jed Ekert as we trekked into the bluffs, hiking through the bushes and the trees into this unknown territory. We climbed some large rocks and found the best path to the top of the bluffs, but that was only half the fun. We knew once we got to the top, we would have a bird's-eye view of whatever game we found to hunt.

Multiple times, Jimmy had to stop and hold both guns so I could climb the next boulder up the hill. At different points in our hunt, we made our own path up the hill to the top of the bluff where we stared across to the bluffs on the other side.

"Where are we going?" I asked.

"Wherever we find something," he explained. I began to wonder if we were wandering, like Dad. He began hiking off down the opposite side of the bluff, down what seemed to be a trail. I followed, hoping to see some sort of wildlife we could hunt. "How many pumps do you have in that?" he asked.

"Five," I explained. I knew that my BB gun only needed about three of four pumps in order to be strong enough to take out a bird.

"Give it five more," he ordered.

"Five?!" I questioned him. "Ten is the most!" I knew my gun would max out at ten pumps and was a little bit afraid of pumping it that many times. I didn't know what kind of damage it could do or how much kick back that might cause when I shot.

"Ssshhhh.... Stop," he shot back. Jimmy stopped. He put up his hand and held a fist in the air like he was leading some sort of Vietnam attack. He lifted his rifle and aimed it off down the hill into the distance. "Do you see it?" he whispered.

"Where?" I whispered back.

"Sssshhhh," he whispered back. Jimmy pulled the trigger and suddenly, I saw a jackrabbit scatter across our path about thirty feet in front of us. It was moving, but something was wrong. It was injured. "I got it!" Jimmy said out loud. "Quick, give me your gun." He reached back and pulled the gun out of my hand as he handed me his. He set my gun up into his shoulder and took close aim again. He squeezed the trigger and that jackrabbit's hind legs went up in the air and landed back on the ground, this time with no movement.

Jimmy took off after it. I followed as quickly behind as I could. When we reached the jackrabbit, we looked down and it wasn't breathing. It laid as still as the rocks and trees around it. Jimmy reached down and grabbed it by its feet.

"Check that out!" Jimmy said as he pointed to the midsection of the rabbit. There was a tiny blood spot in the chest of the rabbit. "Right in the heart," he explained. I looked in amazement at my big brother as he held up his trophy. My brother had just shot a jackrabbit, on the run, with a BB gun, right in the heart and killed it instantly. I was a bit dumbfounded and in disbelief. Never had I thought we would actually be able to kill something besides a bird with our little guns. Jimmy gave both guns to me and carried the jackrabbit.

"What are we gonna do now?" I asked, wondering if we would get in trouble once my parents found out.

"We're gonna skin this sucker!" Jimmy exclaimed excitedly. I wasn't entirely sure what that meant, but it sounded pretty gross. I was sure that was what us men were supposed to do after a hunt though and I went along with it. Jimmy obviously knew what he was doing so I followed his lead. We made our way back over the bluff and through the field, back to our quonset hut house.

We were renting an old quonset hut that had been turned into a house. My parents were either out looking for work or at work. We never really knew which when they were gone. But they were gone and we had freedom to run and play. Terri had been in charge, but now that she was gone, living in a foster home in Indiana, Jimmy was in charge. Of course, we had left Shelby and Shannon at home by themselves to go hunting, but *how much trouble could a five and three year old get into by themselves?* we figured.

When we got back, Jimmy took the rabbit out back behind the house and found a good spot on a large rock to lay it out.

"Wait here, I'll be right back," Jimmy said. He went inside to check on Shelby and Shannon and to get his next most beloved tool, his hunting knife. He came back with his replica version of the *Rambo* knife. It was much smaller than the real thing, but we both thought it was the real thing. Nevertheless, he used it to cut the rabbit wide open.

"Here, hold the legs, like this," he explained while demonstrating how he wanted me to hold the rabbit. I hesitantly held the legs while leaning back and turning my head to the side. "Come on! Hold it up!" he said as he raised his voice, getting annoyed with me. I had almost let it drop back to the ground as I winced, looking away and not sure what to expect. I was hoping he didn't cut me as he intended to butcher this poor, lifeless animal.

I held the upper legs and Jimmy grabbed the lower legs to stretch it out and he began cutting up near the neck, slicing down the length of the body. All seemed well at first and Jimmy really seemed to know what he was doing. Then suddenly, a terrible scent excreted from the body of the dead animal. I looked down and noticed some fur hanging off the body, separating the skin from the carcass. There was a disgusting poop like substance inside a bubble that began pouring out. I dropped the rabbit and ran away.

"Ewww... that's disgusting!" I exclaimed. He hit some sort of pocket on the animal when he was cutting and the smell that excreted from the body was so disgusting that I could not stand it. Jimmy let it drop too and stepped away. He was a bit disgusted, himself.

"Dang it. I guess I hit a gas pocket," he explained. I had no idea what he meant, but he sure seemed to know. That's why I always looked up to my brother. He always seemed to know so much about hunting, fishing, war and all that guy stuff. He had a knack for it and never blinked in the face of tragedy, even when it was an improperly skinned jackrabbit.

We lived in Pine Bluffs for a couple of months into the winter. My mom was about eight months pregnant with my next brother, Jesse when a snowstorm hit the area. That day my dad had been drinking and talking about how much he loved this town, Grover that we had lived in twice. He particularly liked the bar in Grover, which was odd since he rarely drank in bars. It was only about a thirty minute drive from Pine Bluffs so my dad decided to take us all for a ride to reminisce at the bar in Grover, Colorado.

We all jumped into our 1967 Chevy Impala and off we went down the backroads into the snowstorm. The snowfall got worse and worse and the wind was picking up. When the snow blows across the northern plains of Colorado during a snowstorm, it often covers the entire road, so complete that you can't hardly see it.

This particular trip to Grover was unlike many trips. Dad didn't normally drive fast. I guess he was wanting to make it to Grover before the snow got any worse, so he was driving faster than normal; faster than the speed limit. We were definitely driving the backroads, which was typical of his ways, but this particular time, there was a cop on the backroad.

The police lights flashed on and my dad knew he was done for. It had only been a couple of months since we had been taken away into a foster home and now here he was getting pulled over, driving fast while intoxicated in the middle of a snow storm. But Dad was a smart, manipulative man.

"Can I see your license and registration, please?" the cop asked as he approached the cracked window.

"Officer," Dad quickly shot back, "my wife is nine months pregnant and going into labor. We have to get her to the hospital!" The officer looked down at my mom in the passenger seat and examined her situation. While she was only about eight months pregnant, she still looked the part.

"Oh, I'm very sorry! This weather is terrible. Follow me. I'll escort you into Greeley to the hospital," he explained. My dad sighed a sigh of relief and we followed the policeman with his lights and vehicle clearing our path. We drove even faster than before with our new found escort to the Greeley hospital. The policeman wasn't at our car window long enough to even get a whiff of Dad's breath to know he had been drinking. After the long trek into Greeley, the cop led us right to the emergency room of the hospital. We pulled into a parking spot and all got out of the vehicle. The cop escorted us into the emergency room and we all wondered what was going to happen since Mom wasn't really in labor.

Dad walked up to the registration desk with Mom and they began talking to the nurse. The policeman gave us well wishes and headed out the door. Dad turned to Mom and said, "Oh, false alarm. I guess she wasn't in labor after all," and he escorted her out a different door. By the time we reached our car in the parking lot, the policeman was long gone. We jumped in our car and headed off to the bar in Grover.

We didn't stay in Pine Bluffs too much longer after that. Jesse was born in Cheyenne, Wyoming just forty miles from there and then we moved back to Indiana, stopping and living in Cloverdale.

We spent Christmas in Cloverdale, attending church there for a short time; long enough to get help with Christmas presents. I had hoped for a bicycle again so bad that Christmas, but I got a new stereo for what was a Congleton Christmas tradition. Dad loved music so much that he always assumed a stereo was the best gift we could receive. No matter what we asked for, our major Christmas gift was related to music.

Ironically, Jimmy actually got a pellet rifle that Christmas. This was unheard of for two reasons. First, Dad didn't like guns. Second, it wasn't related to music. We weren't there long though before Dad started talking about moving again.

Jimmy decided he didn't want to move again; so he ran away stealing our car at only fourteen years of age. He didn't get far though* and wrecked the car into the median of a split highway. While the police did bring Jimmy and the car home, Dad knew it was only a matter of time before they tried to take us away again so we left town right away, moving back out west, this time to McCook, Nebraska.

McCook was unique for us if only because we attended school in a three-room schoolhouse. Kindergarten through second grade was in one room, third through fifth grade were in a second room and sixth through eighth grade were in the third room. Jimmy, Shelby and I all attended that school, each of us in a different room. It was at this school, I began to dominate the math flashcard lines and excel in the classroom. I also learned what a computer mouse was, in all places at this tiny, rural, antiquated school building in the middle of Nowhere, Nebraska.

I have no idea how I ever maintained any academic aptitude moving from school to school so often, but I did. Back in third grade, I remember learning triple-digit division three times at three different schools. Each school was teaching it when I arrived. I'm sure that reinforced triple digit division for me, but I always wondered what I missed by jumping from place to place. Somehow I was able to not only stay with my grade level, but actually excelled academically (until homework was required.)

Jimmy graduated eighth grade there and Dad was feeling confident again so we moved back to Indiana once more. This time, we moved to Windfall, which is where Jimmy ran away for good at the end of the summer. Jimmy felt bad for leaving, but he just knew he couldn't finish high school living our nomadic lifestyle. It hurt him to leave, but was his only hope. Nevertheless, after Jimmy left, my world was turned upside down.

* (from Jimmy) "I actually was going to Loogootee where Terri was. I stole the car and it was raining hard and I went to stop at a 4-way stop and the car spun out, flying into a cornfield. I smashed the front end where it landed. I ran off and hid in the woods until the car was towed and I thought the police left. I then started walking to Terri's. I had a backpack, my pellet rifle, and my hunting knife. After probably an hour, a car came up behind me and it was a cop. He turned his lights on. He asked me what I was doing. I told him I was coon hunting. He said there was a wreck a couple miles back down the road and the footprints were small at the crash. I admitted to wrecking the car and he hauled me to jail. When we got there, they took my knife, my rifle and about five hundred pellets. I told them where we lived and that we did not have a phone. Then the worst thing that could happen, occurred. He walked me and my stuff to the car and drove me home. It was about 5:00 a.m. when we got to the house and he knocked on the door. Mom answered and then Dad came to the door. The police officer released me and my stuff to them. When he left, I got beat within an inch of my life. I might have deserved that one considering I wrecked our only car. The next day we went and got the car and were able to get it running, but I think it cost like a hundred dollars to pay the tow bill.

Chapter 13

From Baby to Leader (1984 - 1985)

Our first place to live after Windfall was Ault, Colorado–for a second time. My world was just beginning to change, big time. For years, I had been the youngest in the family before Shelby was born. Terri was in charge and played a maternal role when Mom and Dad were both working. When anything bad happened, Terri and Jimmy received corporal punishment (up to forty spankings with a belt) while I, at worst, received five lighter spankings. In addition, Terri and Jimmy often blamed things on me because I rarely received discipline during those days. I was viewed as the baby who was always favored. I was also favored because I was both a cute and cuddly kid. My dad loved to cuddle with us. I had a sensitive nature and I'm sure that my dad caught on to that, feeling sorry for me as the baby at times.

However, after Jimmy and Terri both ran away and began living in foster homes, I was now the oldest kid at home. Shelby, Shannon and Jesse were all born and suddenly I was in charge of three younger siblings at the ripe old age of twelve years. In just a few short years, I had gone from being the baby who could do no wrong to being the leader who could do no right. I was not ready for this leadership role and I didn't want it. But it was thrust upon me and I paid the consequences for not living up to that role. Whenever Shannon or Jesse did wrong, as little ones under five often do, it was typically my fault for allowing it to happen.

This changed everything for me. My view of my dad prior to this, was lovable and cuddly, at least when he was happy and not drunk. My view of my dad after this was hateful and angry at me all of the time, especially when he was drunk. It probably didn't help that I hit puberty right around the same time, amping my emotions and moods.

We were in Ault for a short time and then moved on to Hudson, Colorado. Hudson is where my memories became much clearer for me. Our moving slowed down considerably as we began to stay at each place a little longer. Mom got a job paying claims for a health insurance company, starting at MetLife which was later bought out several times and eventually became United HealthCare. However, she was able to keep the same job all the way through high school and beyond and worked in the same office every time we moved. This is also why most of our moves during this time remained in Colorado and within an hour or so drive of Denver. Dad had a few manual labor jobs the first few years, as well, but Mom's job ended up making the most money and was very stable. We only moved ten more times over the next seven years before I graduated high school.

In Hudson, my friends began to matter much more. In a weird twist of events, I became friends with two of the most popular kids in my grade, Troy and Tony. I was still the quiet and shy kid, but for some reason they befriended me. Troy was the ladies' man who all of the popular girls either dated or wanted to date. He was a good looking kid with dark brown hair, feathered to each side and parted in the middle, reminiscent of a young Brian Bloom. Troy had a nice house, seemed like he came from a bit of privilege and had plenty of friends, yet he invited me over and included me as his friend for some reason.

Tony, on the other hand, lived in the trailer park down the street and his family was Mexican. In Colorado, this was both accepted and not so accepted as numerous Mexicans lived in the area, but, as in many areas, Mexicans were looked down upon by the majority of white people, as poor immigrants. My dad was as racist as any from his generation and hated that I was friends with Tony. He was always on edge when Tony came over to the house and kept a close eye on him to make sure he didn't steal anything. It's ironic though, when I really think about it and our friendship. Tony brought way more to our friendship than I ever did.

I was the new kid in the area and Tony was a popular kid who excelled at sports. He invited me into his life and friendship. Tony had fairly dashing good looks for a sixth grade kid and was well desired by the girls and admired by the guys. We used to play football in the street in front of his trailer park. We also played on the playground at school. Playing football with these guys provided both friends and belonging for me. Tony and Troy made a big difference for me because I was still a small kid and not very athletic, but they included me so I belonged.

Tony introduced me to "high school style" wrestling. I cringe trying to explain "high school style" wrestling because many are not familiar with it. When I mention wrestling, many people think of *WWE* or *WWF* style wrestling or "rasslin'" as some call it. That word makes me cringe too. I only call it "high school style" wrestling to differentiate between *WWE/WWF* style, Olympic style wrestling (which is similar, but yet still very different) and "high school style." There is nothing fake about "high school style" wrestling and it is a very competitive sport. Tony introduced me to this and I liked the idea of it because in wrestling, I was able to compete against other guys my size. I wrestled in the sixty four pound weight class that year.

Tony also provided me transportation to and from practice with his parents. He told me how to sign up. He worked with me outside of practice and he encouraged me all along the way. I got so into it that year that I asked Santa for weights so that I could work on my strength training. Thankfully, Santa really showed up that year and I did get those weights for Christmas! I probably gained two whole pounds in muscle too. While I say I wrestled in the sixty four pound weight class, I actually weighed somewhere around sixty. That may not seem like much weight difference, but there was no one smaller than me. Much of the season, I had to wrestle in my socks because my parents wouldn't buy me a pair of wrestling shoes and street shoes were not allowed. Thankfully, Tony ended up giving me a pair of his old shoes by the end of the season. He had grown up wrestling since he was five years old. In so many ways, Tony gave and gave to me and impacted my life in ways that he would never know.

I lost every single match that I wrestled that year except for the two matches that I *won* by forfeit because there was no one small enough for me to wrestle. While I didn't excel at wrestling at this point, I enjoyed the sport because I felt like I had a chance against guys my size. I had also learned the basics, which were so very important in that sport. The best wrestlers start when they are very young.

I really enjoyed my school at Hudson too since I was friends with a couple of popular guys that included me in their friend groups. I was also friends with a couple of pretty girls, including one that dated Troy. As was typical for my school experience, I excelled in the classroom in Hudson despite our constant moving. At Hudson Elementary, in the sixth grade, there was a plan for every student to memorize every single country in the entire world which included both the location and the correct spelling. We spent the year going over a continent at a time and taking memorization test after memorization test. There were one hundred and sixty five countries in the world at that time and our goal by the end of our preparation was to take one final test to see how many we could get right in one sitting.

"Don't forget next week is our final exam," my favorite teacher, Mr. Ransom told us. We knew all of our preparations for this test were coming to a head very soon. "Your sponsorship lists are due on Monday prior to the test," he explained. We were promised a trip to the Rocky Mountain National Park as our sixth grade trip. The cost of the trip was $42.50 per student. I knew I wasn't going without sponsorship to help pay for it. We were encouraged to go house to house and collect sponsors where they would offer up five or ten cents for each country we got right on the test. If we got one hundred countries right, they would pay five or ten dollars toward our trip. I had collected my sponsor list and though I had gone door to door a lot, my list of sponsors was rather short and the only way I would have enough is if I got at least one hundred and fifty countries correct. This was a feat that many of us aspired to reach. I had also gone door to door in Hudson trying to sell Grit, but wasn't so successful with that either so I was a bit skittish to ask for sponsorship.

"What if we spell it wrong?" a classmate asked.

"Then it is only worth half credit," Mr. Ransom explained. "Typically, only one student out of about seventy five get them all right. Many times nobody can get them all right," he explained. I knew if someone else in our class had a chance, it would be Mary Jane or Jennifer whom I had a crush on. Mary Jane was more my height and blonde, but she had a crush on Troy so I knew I didn't have a chance with her. Jennifer was very tall and had long flowing brown hair. She was both smart and a hard working student. She was definitely one of the smartest kids in class. Troy and Tony didn't have a chance because they didn't care much about school. They did just enough to get by, a tactic I picked up later in school once homework became required.

"Now, before we head out for lunch, I had a note that I wanted to share with everyone." Mr. Ransom explained. Before students could text each other with cell phones, we sent text messages via paper and pencil. The problem with that was, we weren't allowed to do it then either. They were also much easier to intercept than a mobile text message. Mr. Ransom intercepted a note from earlier in the class period that the class wasn't yet aware. "It appears Mr. Delross has a crush on someone and wanted to express it through this little note." He held up a piece of paper folded into a little rectangle. It was folded not in the typical end over end, it was folded in triangles and other awkward shapes only to take on its final rectangular form with a little flap to open it at the edge of the note. I imagine Mr. Ransom shared this information with everyone to minimize the number of notes being passed around class, but we enjoyed the drama with which he displayed. The whole class responded with an, "ewwwweeee" sound just waiting to hear the juicy news.

"I won't tell you the name of the person because that wouldn't be very nice, but her initials are..." he paused for dramatic effect. "Mary Jane." Troy slapped his forehead and Mary

Jane blushed just about as red as possible. The class laughed, the bell rang and we all went off to lunch to play football in the schoolyard. After lunch, I wasn't feeling well so I asked to go to the nurse. When I approached the nurse's office she was helping another student. When she got around to asking what was wrong, I told her that I wasn't feeling well. She called home, but my parents didn't answer because they were both working. She offered to let me lie down in her office. I felt like throwing up, but I never did. I ended up falling asleep on the cot in her office.

When I awoke, her office light had been turned off and she was nowhere to be seen. I laid there for a few moments, wondering what I should do and what time it was. After a bit, I decided to get up and see if she was around the corner in the hallway or another nearby office, but when I stepped out into the hallway, I realized all of the lights were off and the hallway was completely empty. There was no noise. I could hear a pin drop. I noticed the clock hanging on the wall in the hallway above the lockers and it read, 4:05. *What? School got out at 3:15 pm!*

I walked toward the front of the building and looked into the main office. No one was there. I went down the hall and looked into a few classrooms. Everyone was gone! I had fallen asleep in the nurse's office, feeling sick and when I woke up, everyone had forgotten about me and gone home. I decided to go ahead and walk home. I walked out the front of the building and started home.

The afternoon was nice and the sun was shining. I just couldn't fathom how they forgot about me and just let me sleep there. I really liked this school, but they had abandoned me! I passed by Troy's house on the way home so I stopped by. He and a few friends were hanging out. I hung out with them for a few, but finally went home. My parents never even knew what happened. I wasn't going to tell them because I figured I would get in trouble somehow.

The following week, we took our exam of all of the countries in the world. I was ready. I had studied up and I felt really prepared. They handed out large, blank global maps of the entire world with every country identified by shape and had a coordinated space attached to it. They set a timer for one and a half hours. Each of us had two pencils, just in case one broke. I feverishly began writing down every single country, being careful to spell it exactly as I remembered. When I got to the smaller island countries in the Pacific Ocean, I moved a little slower, but still felt fairly confident that I was doing well. I finished in about forty five minutes and began looking over all of my answers to double check my spelling and my memory. I had to get most of them to have a chance at going on this trip!

Finally, I knew I was done and felt pretty confident with most of them so I turned my map in and hoped for the best. Unfortunately, we had to wait a whole day to get our results. I wanted my results instantly! After all, I had an hour and a half to complete the map, why did they get a whole day to give me my results?! But I went home and dreamed about what this trip might be like. We had been through the mountains a few times during our moves, but we never spent any time there and definitely never got to experience it like a tourist with my friends. I loved those friends and they had given so much to me in ways they would never know. It was hard to go from school to school and never know if I was going to be accepted or find any friends.

That night when I got home, Dad told us we were moving again. I was devastated. I had finally found a great group of friends. I had finally found acceptance. I had finally found a sport I loved. My trip to the Rocky Mountains was supposed to be the following week with my class and I hoped I had already earned it! Now, Dad said that we were going to move the weekend before the trip.

"Listen," Dad said, "we are MOVING INTO the mountains! You're not just going to be able to visit the mountains for a week on a trip, but you actually get to live in the mountains. It's going to be beautiful!" Dad tried to convince me that this was better. I was so upset, I just ran to my room, put my face in my pillow and began crying. *Why?! Why?! Why did we have to move now?* I cried myself to sleep that night.

I woke the next day with the anticipation of finding out the results of our test, but knowing that it wouldn't matter in the long run. I arrived in Mr. Ransom's class hoping to hear my results.

"Good morning, class." our favorite teacher greeted us as we all sat when the bell rang. Little bits of conversation continued, but quickly hushed as they realized he had more to tell us. "You all worked very hard this year on our global map test. I was very impressed." He mumbled a bit more, talking about all of our hard work, but I was just wanting him to shut up and give us the results. "This year was different than any year in the past," he explained. "Out of seventy-seven students, FOUR STUDENTS got every single country located in the correct spot and spelled correctly."

What? FOUR STUDENTS?! I bet Mary Jane and Jennifer were two of them! *Could I possibly be one of them?* I wondered.

"Those four students were..." he paused for dramatic effect. "Mary Jane." All of the students clapped. I clapped. "Jennifer." We all clapped again. "Pete." Everyone clapped. "And, Shawn Conjeltun" he said. I was thrilled! I was ONE OF THE FOUR! I had worked so hard and was able to get enough sponsorship money to go on the trip, and proved myself academically. Then, suddenly, reality hit when I remembered we were moving. Everyone celebrated how well the whole class did and the four perfect scores. I stayed silent and smiled a disheartened, fake smile because I knew what it meant for me.

That weekend we moved from Hudson, located outside of the northeast suburbs of Denver and moved into the mountains southwest of Denver on Interstate 285. We passed Aspen Park, Conifer and went further and further into the mountains. Finally, we descended down a large two mile stretch of road which began at the top of Crow Hill. This was a dangerous section of highway where large trucks needed to take extra precaution so that their brakes did not lock up on them as they descended the steep terrain. When we arrived in town with our heavily loaded car, we pulled into one of the first stops on the right into what looked like an old motel.

As we pulled into the parking lot, Dad told us, "this is it." We looked around looking for a house or an apartment, but only saw the hotel. We pulled up to one of the doors on the highway side of the motel. Dad got out first, followed by Mom and then us kids piled out. They walked up to one of the hotel doors, put the key in and opened it. "Home sweet home," Dad said and walked in.

Leaving Hudson and moving to Bailey at that important time seemed pretty typical for my experience, but I was crushed. I was upset and this was the first time that I ever boycotted one of our moves, even if I just did so internally. However, something unorthodox happened for the first time in my transient life.

Chapter 14

Growing Up Quickly (1985 - 1986)

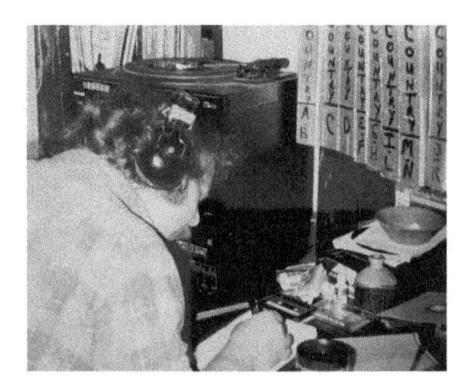

We lived in Hudson, Colorado when I was in sixth grade. I attended an elementary school there, when we enrolled in Platte Canyon School District where I finished sixth grade. I started at Fitzsimmons Middle School, a few miles outside of Bailey. The most unbelievable thing happened to me my first week of school.

My parents actually communicated with my previous school, Hudson Elementary and worked it out for me to go back for the trip with my sixth grade class to Rocky Mountain National Park. My great effort to learn the countries and their spelling actually paid off! I took it upon myself to walk through our little town and collect all of my sponsorship money before we left. I was proud of my accomplishment and I looked forward to the positive feedback from my sponsors when I shared the good news with them.

Mom drove me back from Bailey to Hudson where I was able to catch the bus with my classmates. I attended this one last hurrah with Troy, Tony, Mary Jane and Jennifer! I don't remember any provision ever being made before or after a move for this type of thing for me or any of my siblings. I am still very grateful for that trip and experience with my friends.

Rocky Mountain National Park was everything I imagined. There were large, beautiful, snow capped mountains. The smell of pine emanated from the magnificent, deep green conifer trees. The weather was amazing that week – glowing sunshine and stretching into the seventies. We stayed in log cabins; ate and hiked together; enjoyed all that the beautiful surroundings and mountain lakes provided; skipped rocks across the water; and we hiked some more. We had a great time just being kids and I was able to say my final goodbyes to my friends at the end of the week.

The trip inevitably ended and I returned to my new home, situated in a motel that had been converted into apartments on the main drag in Bailey as you enter from Crow Hill on Interstate 285. Directly behind our apartment was an old-time grocery store called the Bailey Country Store and it looked like a large log cabin. When we entered, we got the sense of what a small town grocery store was like at the turn of the century. There were wooden shelves and many of the products seem to be from an era gone by. We could go up to the front counter and tell them what we wanted. They would go find it for us, bag it up and offer to put it on our weekly tab which we could pay at the end of the week. It was like a scene directly out of *Little House on the Prairie*. We loved to go in and buy the hard candy sticks, particularly root beer flavored. My dad loved the black licorice laces they sold in bulk.

Soon after moving in, Mom gave birth to my youngest brother, Jason. It seemed like it happened rather suddenly. One evening Mom said it was time to go to the hospital. Dad loaded her up, told me to watch my siblings and off they went. A couple of days later, they returned with my baby brother. I really grew up that summer. While I had chores before, my responsibilities grew tremendously. Dad didn't have a job yet, but I was still charged with watching Jason most of the time and making dinner for the entire family. Mom had a lengthy commute into Denver. She drove about six miles to Pine Junction where she would catch the city bus to her office building in Englewood. Her commute was over an hour each way, which is why at the ripe old age of eleven going on twelve, I was charged with cooking dinner for the entire family and having it ready when Mom got home every night.

Dad stayed home from working that summer. He may have done that so that he was available to help with Jason, if necessary. Or maybe he just couldn't find a job. Quite possibly, he may have done it to spend more time with his music. His music collecting really began here. He collected record albums several times and in several places growing up, but this is where his collection really began to take shape. Whatever the reason, he was around all of the time, but I was still charged with taking care of Jason. I changed his diapers, gave him his bottles, took care of him when he was crying and did everything for him when he needed it.

"Shawn!!!" Dad yelled from the other room where he was listening to music at his desk. "Jason's squawking! Take care of it!" he continued.

I had been fiddling with our new Betamax VCR (or Beta, for short). Beta and VHS VCRs came out around the same time and we had chosen to go the Beta route. My friend Tony had a LaserDisc player when we lived in Hudson, but I never even had the chance to watch it. Now we had recently purchased (rented-to-own) a Beta VCR through our favorite Rent-A-Center in Denver. I had figured out how to record whatever I wanted to from TV. I loved horror movies and had discovered Peter Cushing's *Frankenstein* movies. I had been attempting to set the timer to record, *The Curse of Frankenstein* which was playing at midnight that night.

"I'll get him!" I yelled back. I went back to my parent's room and picked Jason up out of his crib. He was crying about something. I noticed his bottle in the crib and it was empty, but he had that bottle just before he went to sleep. He was probably dirty, so I checked that. At his young age, his dirty diapers didn't really smell too bad yet, but I'm sure they weren't exactly fun for him to hang out in either. I put him up on Mom and Dad's bed and grabbed the diaper bag sitting next to the crib. I changed his diaper, still a bit grossed out, but I was starting to get used to it. Then I held him high in my arms and bounced him a little bit.

"How's that little buddy?" I asked, smiling at Jason and hoping he wasn't going to start crying again. He smiled and cooed a bit. *Such a cute kid,* I thought. Too bad he wasn't like that all the time. I walked him out to the living room where Dad was at his desk and put Jason in the playpen near the front door by one of Dad's four foot tall speakers. *California Dreamin* by the Mamas and the Papas was blaring on his stereo. I set Jason down, gave him a toy and put his blankie near his other arm. I quickly exited back to the TV and VCR so that I could finish figuring out how to set the timer to record my movie. Dad was sitting at his desk, which was at the edge of where the kitchen met the living room entrance.

Dad's long, scraggly, and curly brown hair poured over his shoulders. His moustache and beard needed trimmed, but rarely were. I was terrified Dad would get up and give me what I deserved if I didn't have everything taken care of; the kitchen cleaned, Jason happy and dealt with and the bathrooms cleaned too.

Dad was smoking a cigarette and writing something in one of his notebooks. He kept a log in three inch binders that were labeled Rock A-D, Rock E-H, Rock I-R, and Rock S-Z for the musical artists that sang the Rock and Roll albums that he owned. He also had three binders for Country and Western music labeled Country A-G, Country H-O, and Country P-Z.

Dad's love for music was unrivaled. He loved it more than life itself. I had heard him talk about, even fantasize about suicide, offing himself so that he didn't have to deal with life. I heard him threaten to kill my mom more than once. I heard him wish that he could kill someone who made him angry, particularly any one of another race who did him wrong or the most recent president. But I never heard him, ever, say he would give up his music.

At that time, my dad had only two record shelves. They were housed near the entrance to the house where a space had probably been used as a mudroom or a coat closet. Dad's two shelves were made out of old doors that were laid on their side so each was about seven feet long and they were stacked with cinder blocks. Both shelves were full and they totaled about eight hundred record albums, including both Rock and Country flavors. Dad logged the artists in his binders, the songs that charted in the top one hundred on the official music charts and numbered each album on the cover. He played each and every album to ensure it's high quality without skipping even though he carefully inspected his records when he purchased them. Occasionally they would still skip even though he couldn't see any particular damage.

He also recorded them on audio tapes, making mix tapes for listening at a later time. Records weren't typically played for entertaining friends. They were played, categorized, catalogued, recorded and put away on a shelf where it was my responsibility to make sure none of the other kids ever touched them. When we had friends over and Dad wanted to play music for them, he would break out one of his mixtapes and play that rather than the actual albums. Occasionally, he would sell those mixtapes to his friends, but only when he wanted to make a little side money. He didn't want it to be a chore, nor the purpose of his music collection. He collected for the pure love and joy the music brought him.

"Shawn!" Dad yelled again. Oh great, I thought, I didn't even hear Jason crying again. I ran back into the front room.

"What?" I asked. "I just changed him and he was happy a second ago," I pleaded.

"We got new neighbors. Did you notice them the other day?" he asked. I remembered a new couple with a few kids moving into our "apartment complex" directly on the back side of our apartment, across from the Bailey General Store.

"Oh, yeah. I saw that," I answered with much relief that I wasn't about to get my head knocked off.

"Go over there and introduce yourself. Welcome them," he instructed.

I was horrified. As a shy kid, I was afraid to talk to strange kids my own age, let alone an adult I didn't know. I imagined myself knocking on their door, introducing myself and having my mind freeze. *What would I say? How would I act?*

"Do I have to? I don't know what to say," I continued to plead.

"Yes, get your *ss over there. Don't be such a jerk. Go welcome them!" he ordered. I sheepishly walked out the front door and around the back side of our apartment which led to their apartment. We actually shared back walls with each other as our apartments faced in opposite directions. *Why did he want me to do this? Why didn't he do it? He's the friendly one who could talk to anyone. What good was it for a kid to do this?* I was so confused. My heart beat inside my chest and I felt so stupid. I had no clue what I was doing.

My closed fist rasped on the screen door. I hoped and prayed they wouldn't answer. No answer. I knocked again, knowing that Dad would ask about that. I prayed more. No answer. Thank you, Lord. I walked back around to our house and went back inside.

"Well, what did they say?" Dad asked.

"Nothing, they weren't home," I explained.

"Well, you can check again later tonight," he ordered. I sheepishly went back into the other room to work on the VCR hoping all the while that Freddy Krueger or Jason did not live next door.

"Where are you going?" Dad asked. "It's about time to start dinner. We're having pizza tonight!" he said excitedly. Pizza was one of our favorite homemade items. Mom had a recipe that she had passed down for pizza dough and we all loved it! But now it was up to me to make sure it happened. I went into the kitchen and pulled out the yeast, milk, and sugar to get started.

"What are we having on them?" I asked.

"Ham and pineapple on one, hamburger and the works on the other," he said. I loved ham and pineapple pizza! Hamburger, not so much. We never bought pepperoni for pizza, which in my mind was heretical. *How do you make pizza without pepperoni?* Ham and pineapple, that's about it. I looked at the clock and noticed it was already 4:30 p.m. and Mom would be home in an hour and a half. Dad went back to his music at his desk and I got busy in the kitchen while Shelby, Shannon and Jesse played in their rooms.

Later that weekend, I rode my bike around town. I still loved riding my bike and the freedom that it gave me. I met my friend, Jonathan in his trailer park across town and we often rode our bikes together. We had another friend, Matt who lived out of town several miles in a remote mountain home. His parents would bring him and his bike in so that he could ride bikes with us. I was free to ride around town on the weekend since Mom was home and could watch Jason. Matt, who was probably my best friend in Bailey, invited me to his church and youth group across town near Jonathan's trailer.

The youth pastor, Phil was a fun and interesting guy. He was also very nice and friendly. He drove an AMC Eagle Wagon and I always admired that car. It was a mountain car if ever there was one. He worked at a radio station for his day job so I thought it was pretty cool to know a radio personality. Every Sunday night he invited us to his house to watch the movie of the week with the youth group. I don't remember hearing about or learning anything about Jesus while visiting this church and youth group, but I do remember they were nice people and I enjoyed their friendship. I also remember the first time I ever saw *Raiders of the Lost Ark* was at Phil's house with the youth group.

Movies were such a huge part of my life, probably beginning here in Bailey as much as anywhere. We bought a second Beta VCR while we were here for the sheer purpose of recording the movies that we rented. We had to drive a couple of towns over to Aspen Park to rent movies, but when we did, we made it worth our while. Movies cost about a dollar on Tuesdays and we rented about six movies at a time. We went home, connected one Beta to the other with the audio-video cables and recorded two to three movies on each blank Beta tape. This also began our movie collection process that was formalized into notebooks years later. Similar to Dad's record collection, the movie collection grew as we recorded movie after movie, though always much smaller than his record collection.

Horror movies were my favorite as a kid beginning from when I was about seven years old. I don't remember where we lived at the time, but I remember sneaking into the living room underneath where my parents lay on the sleeper couch watching *The Shining* with Jack Nicholson. I was so scared, but I was hooked. I watched *Halloween II* in similar fashion also about the same age. I was enamored with horror movies during this phase of our lives. We rented them and watched them together as a family quite often. While slasher movies like *Friday the 13th* and *Halloween* were fan favorites during this time of the 80s, the movie that most gripped me with fear was when we brought *Nightmare on Elm Street* home. I remember vividly how Freddy Krueger could come from anywhere at any time. He wasn't even limited to our dreams. There was no escaping Freddy!

My infatuation with horror initiated the beginning of my writing career, as well. Just before school started the following Fall, we moved again about ten miles from Bailey to a trailer in Grant, Colorado. We remained in the same school, but my mom added ten more minutes each way to her daily commute. At the beginning of seventh grade, I was able to add a Creative Writing class where I wrote short stories. My first story was a horror narrative entitled, *The Missing House*. In my story our house went missing from one day to the next. It just disappeared. I imagine that may have come from the many houses in our lifetime that went missing from one day to the next as we moved throughout the country.

My second story was titled, *Slumber Party* and depicted a familiar teen romp where these girls decided to have a slumber party and were visited by a vicious killer. Not long after that, we found the movie *Slumber Party Massacre* at that local video store and added it to our collection. I had just missed my chance at stardom by a few years! The majority of my stories were horror themed, but one story that garnered me some attention was not.

Our middle school was named after Jesse B. Fitzsimmons who grew up in the area as a rancher and farmer in the early 1900s. During our time there, Halley's Comet was going to be visible in the night sky. Halley's comet was only visible once every seventy-five years. I wrote a tall tale about how Jesse B. Fitzsimmons lassoed Halley's Comet for our first annual creative writing contest. Amazingly, I won the contest and received a major award for it. This was the beginning of truly believing I could be an author some day.

Even though this latest move to Grant allowed me to stay at the same school, it had its downfalls compared to Bailey. First, I couldn't go to the youth group in Bailey since it was now ten miles away. Second, our move took us to a trailer park at the edge of Grant. Grant, however, wasn't much of a town. There were just a few houses, a few trailers in a park, a store and a bar/restaurant. There wasn't anywhere to ride my bike and no friends to connect with.

The only redeeming characteristic for me was that we continued to rent, watch and collect some cult classics like *Scanners*, *The Evil Dead* and the 1984 version of *The Thing*. My dad's record collection continued to grow as well, now totaling a couple of thousand records housed by four shelves constructed of two by fours and cinder blocks. Like my dad's record collection, our video library and viewing history of horror continued to grow and we built a few smaller shelves for them.

I learned an important lesson in Grant that I will never forget. As I prepared dinner one night when neither of my parents were home, I turned on the oven to preheat it. I was cooking our family favorite pizza again. I continued on the dough, stretching it out across our cookie sheets greased with vegetable oil. I poured on the tomato sauce, sprinkled the oregano and mozzarella cheese on top. I added our favorite toppings and then went to put them in the oven. However, I noticed when I went to put them in the oven that it didn't seem very warm. I set the pizza to the side on the counter and double checked the dial. Yep, indeed it was at three hundred and seventy five degrees.

I decided to pull out the drawer underneath the oven and check to make sure the oven had lit. When I pulled it out and looked up, I didn't see the blue and orange flame I expected. *Of course*, I thought, *the pilot must have been out.* I went and grabbed a piece of paper, lit one end and stuck it in the drawer below the oven reaching into where the flames should be. In the next instant, I heard a loud BOOM as the oven exploded and flames sent me flying across the kitchen. I sat there against the wall. My hair had been singed everywhere on my body. I wasn't really sure what was going on or why the oven exploded. I was stunned. After a bit, I gathered myself, turned off the oven and left the kitchen. I waited in the living room, bewildered and shocked.

My parents came home together not long after and found me. Thankfully, none of my brothers or sisters had been in the kitchen and no one else was hurt. My hair was singed, but my skin was not burnt. I had a headache and I was still out of it. Dad explained that I should have checked the pilot light before I started the oven. He also explained that if the oven didn't light the first time, I should have given it time to air out before I tried to light it. Of course, as he explained it, I felt like I was in trouble. This was typically how I felt every time he talked to me during my teenage years which were now in full effect.

Six months later, in late March that year, we moved out of Grant, out of the mountains and back to the plains of Colorado. While we lived in two towns over that entire year, I was able to attend one school for almost a full year. This was the first time in my life that happened. I attended one school building from April 1985 to late March 1986. Just when I thought we had lived in one of the smallest towns though, we found one even smaller. Then we found one smaller than that.

Chapter 15

Agate, Colorado Pt 1 (1986 - 1987)

Initially, when we moved back to the plains of Colorado, we moved to a very small town called Deer Trail. Deer Trail is the Home of the World's First Rodeo if that tells you anything about the kind of town that it is. Most of the streets in the town were dirt. Not gravel, but dirt. And dusty. The rodeo grounds sat at the northwest outskirts of town and the K-12 school sat at the southwest edge of town. We *settled* down just a few blocks away from the rodeo grounds in a small trailer court nearby. This was where I first began to become a big fan of music myself, as I finished out the seventh grade here.

Deer Trail was a small, public high school that housed a community swimming pool. I only had eight total classmates in my grade at Deer Trail, so coming by friends was a bit more difficult. These small town kids were only into cows or basketball or both. I was not. They had all grown up with each other for the past eight years of school. I had not. However, the one area I may have been able to connect with them was music. Due to my dad's influence, my musical tastes coincided a bit, as my favorite artist was Glen Campbell and I loved the song, "Rhinestone Cowboy." That is, until my older sister, Terri came home.

Terri graduated high school with her foster family the year before and spent the following year at a community college in Indiana. She decided that wasn't for her after her spring term was complete and she returned home to live with us in Colorado for the first time since Christmas of her freshman year of high school. I continued to be the family chef, but Terri helped out also; making pizza and brownies as her *specialty*. Another of our family favorite meals was sausage gravy and biscuits, but Terri introduced us to her version which included chocolate gravy instead. I hated it, but others in the family enjoyed it.

"You've got to listen to some better music!" Terri exclaimed. She hated my Glen Campbell. He wasn't so popular in southern Indiana in 1985 when she graduated high school.

"Well, what else would I listen to?" I responded, not really knowing many artists or band names.

"Johnny Cougar, for one!" she said proudly. "Madonna, Cyndi Lauper, and Bryan Adams," she continued.

"Well, put them on. Let me hear 'em." We had been making pizza for dinner and Terri had just placed the pizza pan in the oven and was getting ready to put some brownies on the upper rack. She placed them in the oven and ran down the hall of our trailer. She went back to her room that she shared with my younger sister, Shelby. She returned with her boombox and a few tapes. She slid a tape in the cassette slot and pressed play. The boombox erupted with, "Girls Just Wanna Have Fun" by Cyndi Lauper and she started dancing all around the kitchen.

Terri had this way of just letting loose. She could fully live in the moment and enjoy music or the company of friends. I couldn't believe the years we had lost without her and I was loving getting to know my sister again. I imagined how much fun she was to hang out with as a friend in high school. She often talked about her friends from that time, confessing stories of their parties and activities. I wished I had been there to experience it with her. I also wondered what it was like to stay in Loogootee and experience a somewhat normal life for four years. The song ended and she stopped dancing.

"Here's another great one," she said as she pulled the tape out of the boom box and replaced it with another. "Summer of 69" by Bryan Adams filled the room.

"I got my first real six string..." Terri began playing air guitar and rocking around the room, singing every word. "Bought it at the five and dime... played it 'til my fingers bled... was the summer of 69!"

Her boombox blared at the top of its lungs. That was the only way to listen to music in our house. We didn't just want to hear the music, we wanted to *FEEL IT*! And feel it, we did.

Terri continued to exchange tape after tape, introducing me to John Cougar Mellencamp's "Pink Houses" and Madonna's "Like a Virgin" and Rick Springfield's "Jessie's Girl" and Toto's "Africa." We jammed and laughed and had a great time. Suddenly, we noticed smoke coming from the oven. We were having so much fun we didn't even notice the burnt smell of pizza and brownies emanating from the kitchen.

"Oh, crap!" Terri yelled.

"Dad's gonna kill us!" I screamed back. Terri opened the oven, grabbed a dish towel off the counter top because we didn't use oven mitts. She quickly reached into the oven with the dish towel and pulled the pizza out. She tossed it onto the counter since the heat was searing through the thin dish towel. Then she quickly grabbed the brownie pan out and threw it onto the counter, as well.

"Oh my gawd," Terri said, "What are we gonna do?!" I stared down at the charred remains of the pizza and brownies and wondered if any of it was edible.

"Do you think we could eat any of it?" I asked.

"Maybe," Terri said and then went into our utensil drawer for a pizza cutter. She pulled one out after scurrying through the drawer for a few minutes.

"Let it cool," I said. "We should try it in a few minutes. We've got to get these windows open and get this smoke and smell out. Dad's gonna be home soon."

We quickly scurried to the windows and rolled them open. The windows opened by a hand roller that you twisted counter clockwise to rotate the window panes up while keeping the bug screens in place, similar to an RV. It didn't provide much relief from the smoke since the window openings weren't very large. I opened the front door and Terri went back to the hallway where a box fan was blowing air through the house. She grabbed the fan, unplugged it and brought it near the front door. We strategically aimed it out the front door and plugged it back in. Smoke began to roll out the door, but we didn't know if it was going to be quick or effective enough.

"Dad's gonna be home soon!" she said, unsure of what would happen. Terri was an adult now and Dad was treating her quite well since we hadn't seen her in so long. But we didn't know how Dad would react when he got home. Terri took her boombox and tapes back to her room and I started cleaning the kitchen of the extra mess. We scurried as quickly as possible, eliminating all of the reasons we might get in trouble besides the burnt pizza and brownies.

"Oh, no!" I shouted, "The flies!" I pointed to the front door as I noticed flies coming in from outside. Flies were extremely prevalent in Deer Trail. And Dad hated flies in the house. Terri closed the front door and started to set the table for dinner. I grabbed the most recent *Denver Post* and wrapped up a couple of sections into a homemade flyswatter. I quickly moved throughout the kitchen and living room swatting every moving thing I could find. I knew I had to get rid of them before Dad got home.

Not fifteen minutes later, the front door opened and Dad stood in the doorway. I sheepishly looked up and nervously wondered what he would notice and how he would react.

"What the h*ll happened here?!!" Dad exclaimed. Terri stood in the kitchen near the front door and responded first.

"Our timer must have broken. We burnt dinner," Terri said apologetically.

"When are you guys gonna get your sh*t together?" Dad asked and shook his head. He walked over to the counter, looked at the scorched pizza and noticed Terri had tried to cut it. He reached down and grabbed the pizza cutter with his big burly hands. He rolled the cutter onto the burnt pizza and started laughing.

"You're gonna need a chainsaw to cut that pizza!" he said. He reached over, grabbed the butter knife on the counter by the brownies and attempted to place it into the hard and blackened brownies. "You got a hacksaw?! We need a hacksaw to cut these brownies!" He laughed. So, we laughed. Our emotions were running rampant inside of us, but we let out a barrage of chuckles.

"Terri, I don't know what they taught you in that foster home, but Shawn had his sh*t together here and knows how to cook. You make Texas Chainsaw Pizza and Hacksaw Brownies!" He just laughed so hard as if it was the funniest thing he ever heard. We laughed with him because we knew this all could have gone down so very differently.

We spent a couple of months in Deer Trail, finished the school year there and then promptly moved twelve miles down the road to an even smaller town called Agate. Apparently, Mom's hour-long drive into Denver for work wasn't long enough and we needed to add another fifteen minutes each way to her commute.

Agate was so small, it consisted of only four square blocks. It had a Post Office, gas station and a K-12 school. That was it besides the few houses that completed the four blocks.

We moved into a trailer directly across from our school principal and catty corner to the school. This was across the main street that entered town from the highway. The grass was tall and stringy in our yard and looked as if it hadn't been mowed in years. The trailers we lived in over the years were all pretty much the same to me, but this one had an extra bedroom. This was great since we had one more person with us now that Terri had come home.

Dad got a job at the grain bin in Agate and began working again so Terri and I were left to watch Shelby, Shannon, Jesse and Jason all summer. Dad's record collection continued to grow and he now owned over five thousand albums. He built large shelves out of two by fours specifically for his records. The record shelves took up an entire wall on the right as we entered the trailer. He now had twelve to fifteen binders for each genre of music, both Rock and Country. He even started a binder for Jazz, which he categorized separately. In the center of the record shelf, was a space he left for our TV and VCRs.

We now had seven VCRs in the house (three full sets for recording from one to another) and four TVs, one in each bedroom and one in the living room. We moved onto the VHS formatted video since that format allowed us to record up to four movies on just one tape. VHS formatted tapes had also grown in popularity and were slightly cheaper and more available to rent. While some video companies had found ways to block us from recording their tapes when we rented them, we found ways around that by recording from Beta to VHS or vice versa. Our movie collection grew beyond the initial hundred or so movies on fifty some Beta tapes. We expanded it to three or four hundred movies on a hundred or so VHS tapes.

While Dad was now working during the week at this time, he still found time on the weekends to head into Denver to go shopping at Wax Trax, his favorite record store in the downtown area. We would also hit up Goodwill and Salvation Army stores so that Dad could add to his record collection and we could buy whatever we wanted with our allowance. We did our school shopping there, as well. I'll never forget the find of the century when I was able to procure a pair of black Parachute pants lined with zippers from top to bottom. I loved those pants and felt so in style when I wore them! Periodically, I was also lucky enough to find a pair of Bugle Boy pants and I thought I was *the stuff*. I never dared let any of my friends know that I found them at a second hand store though.

During the weekdays in the summer, we had a lot of both freedom and responsibility. While Terri and I had to watch the younger siblings, we also had little supervision from anyone else during the day. Terri was the closest thing to an adult, now at almost twenty years old, but she was full of fun and Dad still held me mostly responsible. Jason, my youngest brother was one year old, Jesse was nearly three and Shannon was now six. I did not enjoy keeping track of those three little guys nor was I very good at it. I was only thirteen and didn't do a great job since I was focused on running around and having fun myself. Shelby turned eight that summer and wasn't much of a responsibility for me, but I was in charge and had to make sure everyone completed their chores. If anything was left undone, it was all on me.

"Get back in here!" Terri yelled at me.

"No, I'm going to Ronnie's house," I yelled back as I bounded down the steps from the front door and hopped on my bike.

"This house is a mess," she said, "Dad's gonna be p*ssed." She was doing her best to get me to take responsibility and make sure everything got done and I was leaving it up to her even though it wasn't really her job. She followed me out the front door and reached me as I stood my bike up and pulled my leg over the center bar readying myself to take off.

"Stop, you have to stay here and watch these kids and get your chores done," she pleaded again.

"There is plenty of time before they get home. I'll be home later to get it done," I explained. She raised her hand over her shoulder and swung it down to hit at me, but I reached my hand up and smacked the face of her palm with mine as it came down. Though Terri was almost twenty years old, she was even smaller than me at just under five foot and a hundred pounds.

As our hands smacked, I said, "alright, good job!" I laughed, grabbed my handle bars and took off down the dirt street to my friend's house. Terri was so livid, but couldn't do much to stop me. I spent the day playing at Ronnie's house. He was only in fourth grade which was four grades below me, but he was only two years younger than me. He acted much older and we were closer in size than kids my age. I didn't exactly have many options for friends in our tiny town. We were also friends with the kid next door to Ronnie who was the same age as Ronnie, but in sixth grade. We ran around playing Cowboys and Indians, climbing trees, and riding our bikes to life's content. After enjoying my day, Ronnie turned and asked me a question.

"We're having dinner. Want to stay? What time do you have to be home?" he asked. I froze. Suddenly, it hit me.

"Oh, my gawd. What time is it?" I asked.

"It's almost five thirty," he answered.

I was dead. I just knew it. Dad got home around 5:30 and I wasn't even home yet. My chores weren't done and I'm sure no one else's were either. Dinner wasn't even started. I hadn't done anything I was supposed to do.

"Nope, gotta go!" I said as I jumped on my bike and raced the three blocks back to our trailer.

As I pedaled faster than I had ever pedaled in my life, my mind raced with all of the things Dad was going to yell at me for and how I was going to get beaten to death. I just knew it was going to be the end of the world; my world anyway. The wind blew through my hair and I wondered if I would be alive that same time the next day. I imagined all the things my brothers did that I was going to get into trouble for. I could see my sister, Terri sitting back, but not laughing as you might expect from someone with a right to say, "told you so," but crying because she was so sensitive and never wanted us to go through what she went through. I wondered if she would get in trouble too, even though she was an adult and it was totally my fault. My life flashed before my eyes as I wondered if I would ever be allowed to hang out with Ronnie again.

As I reached our trailer, I pulled my bike up to the back door and snuck inside the trailer, hoping to escape discovery if Dad was already home. I hadn't noticed if his car was there so I quickly scurried down the hallway from the backdoor that was situated near the end of the trailer. I peered down the hall and around the corner as I got closer to the kitchen.

"There you are, you little piece of sh*t," my dad said as I rounded the corner. "Where the h*ll have you been? Why is this room so filthy? Where's dinner?" My dad started smacking dishes around the room that were left out and dirty. I ducked and blocked whatever was coming toward me, not knowing if they were aimed at me or coming at me randomly.

"I was out back. I thought this was already clean," I claimed, clamoring for any answer that may seem feasible. I could now hear Jesse and Jason crying in the front room. Terri was sitting with them on the couch. Shelby and Shannon were nowhere to be seen.

"Look at this sh*t! Dirty dishes everywhere! Sh*t all over the floor! What have you been doing, you good-for-nothing piece of sh*t?!!" I cringed and buckled down wondering if he was going to just start swinging. "Get me the broom," he yelled. I lost it. I immediately began crying uncontrollably.

"No!!! Dad!!! Not the broom! I'm sorry! I'll clean it up right now!" I pleaded.

"Get me that d*mn broom or I'll use my hands. Do you want me to get out my belt?!" he screamed. Those two alternatives got me and I quickly moved to the kitchen closet, grabbed the broom and handed it to him.

"Lay over that chair," he yelled while directing me to the kitchen chair.

"Noooo!!!! Dad," I continued to plead, but also began to lay over the chair. I started to reach my hand back as the broom swung toward my rear end. The wood handle of the broom brushed up against my hand and wrist striking them, but barely. The soft end, so to speak, of the broom struck my back end and I lurched forward in the chair moving it a few inches forward.

"One!" Dad yelled. I started to turn toward him and begged him to stop. "Turn your *ss round or your gonna get hit in the head," he yelled. Fear struck me deeper and more present than ever. I turned back around and accepted my fate. "Two! Three! Four! Five!" The broom cracked at my backside four more times and then stopped. I lay there sobbing incessantly. I could no longer hear Jason or Jesse, nor could I tell if Terri was crying, but I'm sure all three were happening. I shut down inside and just sobbed internally, hoping it was all over.

"Now get your *ss up and clean this house! You're going to do Shelby's and Shannon's jobs since you can't seem to do your own or make sure they get them done. That means the bathroom, the living room and the entire kitchen. Then make dinner! You're not going anywhere for a month! You're grounded!" he yelled.

The life that flashed before my eyes on my way home, flashed again and I knew it was gone. Of course, at that moment, I also knew that Dad would feel sorry for me the next day and unground me. It never stuck. He got angry in the moment, laid out his extreme consequences for my failures and then later felt sorry for me and retracted whatever consequences were left.

This same scenario repeated itself several times that summer. I was a slow learner and was more concerned about hanging with my friends before taking care of my responsibilities or my siblings. My friends were an escape from my reality and I preferred hanging with them, regardless of any fear of consequences. Terri and I grew closer as she shared her musical interests with me. I spent more time with her as if we were making up for lost years. However, I still did my best to leave her with my responsibility of cleaning and watching my siblings. She didn't really have to accept them. Sometimes she did, sometimes she didn't.

That fall, I started my eight grade year at Agate. Agate was a public school and bussed students from far out in the county. However, it didn't help much in terms of increasing our school size. When I started the eighth grade, there were only forty-two students in the entire school, kindergarten through twelfth grade. I had only three students, including me in my eighth grade class. My classmates were one boy and one girl. We had five in the seventh grade, which was great because that allowed us to field sports teams. Girls were allowed to play on the guys teams because we didn't have enough to field a team otherwise. Consequently, guys were also allowed to play on the girls teams for the same reason.

I played girl's volleyball that Fall after we moved in. I learned the game and loved it. I was a pretty tiny kid so I didn't have any advantage over the girls on the team. When basketball season arrived, two girls played on our guy's basketball team and they both started over me. This was the first time I had ever played basketball, but I was loving it. Every day I went over to the school and shot baskets on the outdoor court. I fell in love with the game! I wasn't very good and I was too small even compared to the girls on our team, but I still enjoyed it. We barely made it through basketball season though, before our number was up and we ended up moving back east to Illinois after the season.

Dad had introduced some young man to my sister Terri and they started dating almost immediately. Before long they got married and Terri moved out. Gary, my new brother-in-law, already had a trailer in Deer Trail so she moved in with him, of course. Gary was a tall, skinny and likable guy. He was a bull rider at the Deer Trail Rodeo. He wore large belt buckles, *Wranglers* and button up western shirts. He treated Terri well at first, but he drank quite a bit too. He told tall tales with the best of them and loved to hear himself talk. Before long, Terri and Gary were having problems and she decided to leave him.

Dad always tried to convince us a move was for the best. He tried to persuade us that we were moving close to Grandma and Grandpa again (both sets of grandparents lived in northern Indiana). If that wasn't enough, he told us that we were moving closer to Jimmy who was still living in a foster home in Loogootee at the time. This time he may have tried to convince me that a different school would have wrestling. Or he may have tried to tell us that we needed to move for Terri's sake so that she could get away from Gary. Whatever he used to manipulate us into thinking that moving was a great idea, we were all in (as if we had a choice) and we headed back east, arriving first in Waterman, Illinois. We weren't back east for long, but that summer I worked my first real job and then our lives changed forever once we returned to Agate.

Chapter 16

Agate, Colorado Pt 2 (1987 - 1988)

Mom transferred her insurance job to Aurora, Illinois which was a distant suburb of Chicago. We moved into Waterman, a small village with a population of about a thousand and a total area of one and a half miles. Northern Illinois was quite different from Colorado where we had lived for three years. The dryness and deadness of Colorado made way to the greenness and botanical life of Illinois. Large, green maple trees lined the streets and green grass was everywhere. In Colorado, it seemed that most decent sized trees only grow near rivers and grass required constant watering. Waterman, however, was full of green plant life; it was like the Garden of Eden!

I started watching sports on TV during this era of my life. Dad watched the Cubs almost every day and I often joined him learning about Andre Dawson, Ryne Sandberg and Shawon Dunston. The Cubs weren't great that year, but I also learned they weren't great for a lot of years, having won their last World Series in 1908. I learned how much my grandparents loved the Cubs and how Dad's mom watched them everyday on her console television. Dad taught me the history of the team and that Cub fans everywhere have held out hope for another World Series, no matter how many bad seasons they have endured. *True fandom requires this kind of hope*, he told me.

School life helped me connect with Chicago sports in two additional ways. During this time, Magic Johnson and Larry Bird were the premiere players in the NBA. All of my classmates were talking about a third year player that was exploding on the scene with high profile scoring in Chicago. The debate about who was better, Magic or Larry, was being interrupted with staunch opinions that Michael Jordan was now the best player in the NBA. I started to watch the Chicago Bulls to see what everyone else was talking about. I quickly agreed with them and became a huge Michael Jordan fan, like much of America. We loved catching his Mars Blackmon commercials and dreamed of owning a pair of his shoes.

I took shop class for the first time in Waterman where I made a pair of Chicago Bears bookends. I had actually become a bit of a Bears fan when we lived in Grant, Colorado. We watched them defeat the New England Patriots in dominating fashion in Super Bowl XX. Sweetness, as they called Walter Payton, was easy to root for, as well as the mouthy and brash Jim McMahon. Watching their Super Bowl Shuffle video was a lot of fun and I was easily endeared. I became a much bigger fan of the Bulls and Cubs than the Bears. Michael Jordan always made it a lot of fun to watch basketball as the most dominant scorer in the game. He was such a flashy player and premiere defender.

Terri moved with us to Illinois since she had decided to leave her husband Gary. We continued to listen to music together and enjoy our time as we were learning new music together for the first time with songs such as "I Just Died In Your Arms" by Cutting Crew, "Jacob's Ladder" by Huey Lewis and "Looking For a New Love" by Jody Watley. We danced around the kitchen and talked and laughed about music. Then, one day Terri came in from the front porch where she had been on the phone.

"What's wrong?" I asked her. She had obviously been crying.

"Nothing. I was just talking to Gary," she replied.

"Was he being a jerk?!" I asked, figuring he did something to make her cry.

"No." She paused. "I can't stay. I'm going back. Gary and I are getting back together. I miss him and we have to make this work," she explained.

Suddenly, my mind went somewhere else. I was going to lose my sister again. We had lost her for five years while she was in high school and her first year of college and now she was leaving us again. I felt like I had just gotten her back and we were having so much fun together.

"When are you going? Does Dad know?" I asked.

"Probably next weekend. Gary is coming to get me. No, I haven't told Dad yet. I don't know how he'll respond," she said. While Terri was leaving and I was not looking forward to it, ultimately it didn't seem like that big of a deal in the moment. I lost her once and moved on, just like I had done with every friend I ever had. *This wouldn't be that big of a deal*, I thought. Terri left the following weekend and I graduated eighth grade a few weeks later.

One day, about a month later, I put on Huey Lewis and the News' album "Fore!" and laid on my bed enjoying the music. Suddenly, it hit me how much I missed my sister. My eyes filled with water and I just laid there for an hour, crying, because I had lost my sister again and I still wasn't able to see my brother, Jimmy. Terri and Gary reconciled so she stayed back in Colorado. Jimmy lived in southern Indiana and we were in northern Illinois. We never even went to visit him once. I think Dad was afraid to take us back into Loogootee for fear that they would try to take us away from him permanently. He never paid any child support for them either, which technically made him a "wanted man" in Indiana.

After just a couple of months in Waterman, we decided to move to Ransom. Mom had about a forty-five minute drive into Aurora for work in Waterman, but now her drive was extended to almost an hour and fifteen minutes again. Ransom was further out and an even smaller town than Waterman.

I liked Ransom for a couple of reasons though. First, I got a job detasseling corn that summer. Local farming companies hired young teenagers to detassel corn for minimum wage. That was my first real job and I spent the summer walking through the corn field, pulling the tassels off corn stalks. The tassel is the top portion of a corn stalk that feels like a beaded rope. As we walked through the corn field, we inspected each corn stalk and pulled the tassels. While I only made $3.25 an hour, we worked long hours; as many as fifty to fifty five hours a week. I made quite a bit of money for a young guy with his first job. It was hot and I was sweaty, but I enjoyed the sun and the work was well worth the money.

The second reason I enjoyed Ransom is, I took some of that money and bought myself a three-wheel homemade dragster. This was not like an ATV (All-Terrain Vehicle), but was more like a dune buggy. I rode that three-wheeler all over that small town because there were no local cops to keep me in check.

One weekend, Mom and Dad left town with all of the kids. They allowed me to stay back since I was thirteen going on fourteen and I convinced them that I had to work and I would be okay by myself. For some reason that summer, it seemed that all of the kids I worked with in the corn fields smoked cigarettes. Some even smoked pot, which got them fired when they tried it on the job. Whatever it was though, I decided I wanted to try smoking for myself, to fit in, I suppose.

The day after my parents left, I went into my dad's desk drawer and pulled out his Swisher Sweets. Little did I know, these were not actually cigarettes. They were little cigars, but they looked just like cigarettes. All of the kids joked about how other kids fake smoking by not inhaling so I knew I needed to do it right. I found a pack that had already been open because *certainly Dad would not realize one missing from an open pack,* I thought. His lighters were also in the drawer and I pulled out a Bic lighter. I put the cigar in my mouth and lit the lighter. I drew the flame up to the end of the cigar and took a deep breath, breathing through the cigar with my lips held tightly together. As I did, the cigar lit and I began choking on the smoke that entered my lungs.

Don't be such a wuss, I told myself and after I stopped choking, I took another puff. This caused me to cough a second time, but was much more manageable and expected. I drew the smoke deep into my lungs and held it for a couple of seconds before releasing. I did my best to mimic my dad's smoking example, but I had little idea what I was doing. I continued for a while even though my chest began to burn and it tasted disgusting. But I kept going because I needed to know for myself what this was all about. *After all, if it stays this bad, people wouldn't do it,* I told myself, assuming it would both taste better and hurt less. It didn't. I smoked a full half of that cigar, gave up and smashed the rest into my dad's ashtray on his desk.

It was so disgusting and my chest hurt for three days afterwards. I decided from that moment on that I would never smoke. Years later, I found out that I had actually tried a cigar, not a cigarette, but that didn't matter. My one time experiment was over and I decided I was not a smoker. I disposed of the evidence, then enjoyed the rest of my weekend alone as much as I could with my three-wheeled dragster. Not long after my parents returned, we moved again. This time to Streator, not too far away, but a much larger town. It added another five to ten minutes to Mom's daily commute.

We lived above a downtown grocery/drug store and we weren't there but a few weeks before Dad decided he had enough of Illinois and living out east for the last time. The summer was coming to an end and he wanted us to be back in Colorado for the start of the school year. I'm not sure how, but my guess is he convinced us that we needed to live near Terri again since things were still going well for her and Gary and she was planning to stay there. As it turned out, Terri found out she was pregnant while we were in Waterman, which led to their reconciliation and desire to work things out. She kept that part a secret for a while, but she was due in September and I'm sure Dad wanted to be near his first grandchild so we moved back to Agate, Colorado.

We arrived back in Agate just a few days before school and moved into a house on the backside of the same block our trailer had been on. I started ninth grade at Agate High School where my class size had almost doubled. We now had five students in the ninth grade, including myself. We had a total of seventeen students in the entire high school. High school sports there remained gender based though. Guys did not play on the volleyball team since we had enough to field a team. Guys did; however, play six-man flag football as a fall sport. While my small stature didn't matter as much in flag football as it would have in tackle football, I still found myself on the non-playing end of a sport. We had eight guys that played and I suppose as a freshman who was both tiny and slow, I expected to not be allowed to play much.

One Saturday in the early Fall, my parents decided to go shopping in Denver without us kids. They decided to go with some friends in their car. Dad never really liked to put the miles on our cars since Mom was already doing that for her daily commute. On the way home, they decided to take a drive through the country. Most backcountry roads in Colorado are dirt and they are barely wide enough to fit two vehicles since they are so rarely traveled. Most people drive in the middle of the road and then get over to the side when someone is coming from the opposite direction.

Apparently, as the story is told, Mom and Dad were riding in the back seat of their friend's vehicle. They were driving on a secluded dirt road approaching the crest of a hill. Another vehicle on the opposite side of the hill was driving in the center of the road and as they approached each other from opposite directions, neither vehicle was aware of the other. At the crest of the hill, both vehicles swerved, but it was too late and they slammed into each other. Dad was sitting in the backseat sideways in a more relaxed position and, of course, was not wearing a seatbelt. Mom was directly behind the passenger seat facing forward, wearing her seatbelt. While the accident did fairly significant damage to the vehicles, the worst human injury was Dad's leg.

Dad was taken to the hospital and treated for a left leg injury. They returned home late that evening with the accident being completely unbeknownst to us at the time. Dad hated hospitals and all that his treatment would have entailed and he refused to do any physical therapy afterwards. His leg has never fully healed. Dad never worked a job again after that. While Mom had already become the breadwinner for the family, Dad had still worked a few physical labor jobs in the previous few years. However, that was now behind us since he was never able to physically recover or even walk without a limp again. Ironically, I heard years later that the driver of the other vehicle had been drinking.

Dad became a full-time stay-at-home Dad, but focused mostly on his record collection at his desk rather than taking care of any kids or doing household chores. All of the chores continued to be the responsibility of us kids, including making dinner. Dad's responsibility was yelling at us when we didn't do something or yelling at us to do something.

I'm not sure why I continued to participate in sports that I was rarely given the opportunity to actually play in a game, but I suppose it was better than being at home. When the winter season arrived, unfortunately, they did not offer wrestling due to being such a small school. For Agate, basketball season had arrived, I decided to play again hoping I had a chance because there were only eight players on the team, including myself. However, I was still not quite five feet tall and not even a hundred pounds. On game days, I had to roll my warm up pants multiple times. One time I even slipped on them going up for a warm up layup as the too long pant leg slipped underneath my black Converse hightops.

Our team was led by the Padilla boys. Both Larry and Rich were nearly six feet, three inches tall. We called them the twin towers and when they were both playing, we were hard to beat. Most everyone on the team was a solid athlete except for one other nerd boy like myself who I'm guessing his parents made him play. But I worked hard and did my best. I even wanted to demonstrate my toughness and tenacity by not drinking water during practice. Little did we know in the eighties how important staying hydrated was, but no one *made* me drink and I was foolish enough to think that was a good thing. I enjoyed the game during practice and dreamed of my chances to play and one day become like Michael Jordan. I would often do silly things like stick my tongue out when I drove to the basket to mimic my idol.

One Saturday afternoon in early December, Mom and Dad went into Denver to go to Wax Trax and Goodwill stores, shopping for Dad's record collection. Us kids stayed home again this time and played around the house. I figured they were probably Christmas shopping and I was just happy about that. We spent the afternoon watching movies and hanging out. I went into my room to listen to Van Halen since I had just gotten their latest tape called *5150*. I spent the afternoon in my room listening to my tapes.

"What the h*ll is going on in here?!!" my dad yelled from the living room. I had fallen asleep lying on my bed listening to my Sony Walkman. It must have shut off at the end of the tape. As I came to, I quickly tried to ascertain my whereabouts and situation. It hit me that Mom and Dad were home and I had no idea what my younger siblings had been doing. I came running out of my room, past the record shelf and into the living room.

"What? What happened?" I asked. Dad was standing over his desk, looking at his stereo that sat on it.

"Who the h*ll has been messing with my stuff, Shawn?!" Dad yelled. He was fiddling with his tapes and his open tape decks on his stereo.

"I don't know. I didn't do anything," I explained. I could tell several tapes were strewn across his desk as if they were just tossed in the air and landed there.

Dad always kept his space immaculate and orderly. We were barely allowed in his space and only when we were in his presence. Suddenly, Dad noticed a pile of records out of place on the floor near his desk. There were stacks of records on or near his desk all the time. That was part of his process for going through his records; recording them in his binders, playing them to ensure top condition and cataloging them before they went on the permanent shelves. However, I didn't know the difference between that and what I was looking at, except that

I now noticed that several albums were out of their sleeves and laying directly on the ground. Suddenly, Dad did too.

"You son of a b*tch! I can't believe you let them into my stuff! You are fourteen years old and you can't watch them little b*st*rds! What the h*ll??!!" Dad continued to yell while inspecting the damage that Jason and Jesse must have created while I was sleeping and listening to my music.

"Oh my gosh," I exclaimed, trying to agree with my dad as if I was on his side. I looked over his mess that my brothers had created and wondered just how bad he was going to react. This was the ultimate though. Dad was most angry when I let my brother's mess with *his* stuff. As I looked over the mess, I saw my dad's hand come flying by my head. I quickly responded by getting my hand up by my head to block his blow, but it still landed with force knocking my hand into my own head and I went flailing several feet.

"Get the broom! I'm tired of this sh*t!" Dad yelled. I went quickly into the kitchen for the broom thinking that the broom would be getting off easier than I might get otherwise this time. As I turned around with it to return, Dad was already upon me. He grabbed the broom out of my hand, snagged me by the collar and pressed my face against the wall. "Don't move!" he continued. He stepped back, grabbed the broom by the end of the handle and swung a long swing around, striking my lower back with the "soft" portion of the broom. I thought about trying to block it with my hand, but remembered the last time my hand and wrist were contacted with the broom. I burst out in loud tears as the broom struck me a second time, this time making contact with my upper rear end. Three more swats and I crumpled to the floor crying.

"Jim! Stop it!" Mom screamed.

"Go to your room!" Dad yelled. I quickly went back through the kitchen and the living room to my bedroom and closed the door. I threw myself on my bed and laid there and cried for what seemed like forever. For the next couple of hours I could hear my dad and mom fighting. I wasn't sure where the other kids were. I assumed they were probably huddled up and hiding behind their bedroom doors. After a while, I fell asleep.

"Shawn, come out here," my dad said to me through my doorway. I was waking up, but not really sure what was going on. I sheepishly rose and entered the living room through my bedroom doorway. I didn't say a word. Dad had calmed down and was more settled in his voice. "Come on out here," he said as he walked me out to our car parked half in the yard, half in the street. Dad got in the driver's side and I followed suit on the other side, setting in the passenger seat, remaining quiet. Dad had a twelve pack of Schlitz beer sitting on the floor by my feet.

"Hand me one of those," he said. "We had a rough day today. Mom and I were arguing all day. I hate arguing. I never know when we should move and when we shouldn't. Sometimes, I'm really just a f*ck up. I love your mom. I love you kids. I don't tell you this enough, but I'm proud of you. I know that I never come to your sporting events, but I'm really proud of you. I would come more if I knew you were playing, but don't think that doesn't mean I don't love you. Do you know what was in the back of the car when we came home?"

I stayed silent.

"Your Christmas, that's what was in the back of the car. We got you a large boombox for a hundred and fifty dollars AND we got you a stereo for your room which ALSO cost a hundred and fifty dollars. We got over three hundred dollars worth of stuff to show you how much we love you..."

He rambled on and on about what a good kid I was and how much he cared for us all while he finished off the twelve-pack of beer. He sounded honest and real, but I didn't buy it. *He didn't love us. He didn't have a clue what love was. Love is not a gift or even multiple gifts when you treat your kid like crap and barrage him with negativity about himself,* I thought. *Dad lived for himself and every decision was based on what he wanted. He was so manipulative and I just wished he never existed in my life.*

The next morning when I woke up, Mom told us to start packing our stuff. Dad was gone somewhere at the time and she said that she had enough and was going to finally leave him. She had boxes for us and we all got started with hope in our hearts. *Could it be that we could finally escape his grasp? Could it be that we could find the life we had always hoped for?* We spent the next several hours packing and wondering what was in store for us. Later that afternoon, while we were still packing, we heard Dad come in the house. More fighting and yelling ensued. During the fight, Dad took all of Mom's work clothes out of her closet and literally cut them up with a knife. He was jealous of her job and tried to prevent her from leaving him. We all stayed in our rooms while they fought and fell asleep without any idea of what the next day would hold.

The following day when I woke, I went out into the living room. Mom and Dad were sitting on the couch with the newspaper. They didn't say much, but they sat there as if nothing had happened. Mom had usually gone on to work by now, but was sitting on the couch as if it was the weekend.

"Go ahead and get ready for school, you're gonna be late," Dad said. I went back to my room and got into my boxes to get some clothes out for school. There was never another mention of the weekend again. Mom never left Dad. We never left Dad. We stayed in that h*llhole of a home and continued on. Until March, when we decided to move closer to metro Denver so that Mom didn't have to drive so far. We left Agate and moved into the suburbs where I would find my greatest hope to date.

Chapter 17

Northglenn, Colorado (1988 - 1989)

Technically, we moved to Thornton, which was the street address at our apartment complex, but I attended Pecos Jr. High to finish out the ninth grade and then Northglenn High School in the tenth grade. We moved into an apartment complex in Thornton on the third floor. This was the first time that we really lived in a big city even if it was the suburbs of Denver. It was also the first time that we really lived in a large apartment complex. Mom had a close commute though. She was driving to the other side of Denver, but it was only about a half-hour commute. I developed some good friendships there with others who lived in our apartment complex.

Because of Michael Jordan and my two years of playing in Agate, my love for basketball had grown. Our apartment complex had two luxuries that I loved. The first was the nice outdoor basketball court in the commons area. I spent so many hours everyday shooting baskets where I developed a friendship with a twenty-three year old black man named Kevon. The other was the pool, which allowed us to go swimming every day in the summer for free.

Kevon taught me some things about the game as we shot around together. He didn't treat me like some scrawny fifteen year old kid, but he treated me as an equal friend. I thought this was odd, not only due to his age, but he was about six foot one and could slam the basketball. I had no skills compared to him, but he befriended me and let me play with him and whoever else showed up. He also invited me into his apartment where we watched the tough playoff games between the Bulls and the Bad Boys of Detroit, also known as the Detroit Pistons. He also allowed me to stick around after the game when he and his friends started smoking pot.

That wasn't the first time I smelled that terribly pungent odor, though. When I was detasseling corn in Illinois, several other workers got fired for stopping in the middle of the corn field and smoking it. *What a terrible smell*, I thought. Trying to smoke Dad's Swisher Sweets had been bad enough, I only imagined how terrible it was to smoke marijuana. I never took a puff at Kevon's apartment, though I stuck around for maybe thirty minutes. I was familiar with the possible second-hand effects and decided to leave his apartment even though I never actually felt them.

I had a few other friends in that complex, as well. Lorena lived directly across the hall from Kevon. She was close to my age and had moved there from New York. She carried a strong accent and was a lot of fun. She wasn't attractive to me so I wasn't interested in her that way, but we hung out often and she had this way about her that was bold and daring. Billy was another one of my apartment friends and we were the same age. Billy was a bit of a nerd, but he was the only guy my age that lived there and befriended me. Billy was a fan of the Denver Broncos as I'm sure many others were, but I had an affinity for the Steelers and the Bears even though I never actually watched football.

Billy was my friend that introduced me to Heather and Tara. These two girls also lived in the apartment complex and were extremely attractive. We hung out with them a lot, even though neither of them really showed much interest in me beyond friendship. I was enamored with them and couldn't take my eyes off of them. I was just amazed that they would even be my friend. We swam at the pool together a lot which was also a great bonus, watching them in their bikinis. It's probably not news to you that teenage guys like to look at teenage girls.

I grew up in many ways here. While I asked Heather out several times and she denied me, she did take time to think about it. Tara was the one I was most enamored with. I just knew she was even further out of my league. One day, Billy told me that Heather was willing to teach me how to french kiss. I couldn't believe it. I just knew he was making it up. But Heather confirmed and eventually it happened. I thought I grew up that day and became a man. I also learned for the first time what "mooning" was when the two girls gifted Billy and I from Heather's third floor apartment. I always thought it was rather a weird thing for someone to do and never really understood why they did it. It seemed like it was supposed to be a mean thing, but not from these girls. It never went further than these two experiences, but I felt like I had grown up a lot that summer. I still had no idea what it meant to be a man.

I first attended Pecos Jr. High School from late February to May of that year. I actually went back to junior high after being in Agate High School in the ninth grade. It only lasted a few months though and I actually started at Northglenn High School that summer, not for academics, but a couple of different athletic programs. They had a summer basketball league, which I promptly joined. I finally felt like I had developed some skills and was able to compete in that league even though I was still pretty small. I remember playing for several weeks and feeling like I might be able to make the team the following year. But then the *other* sports program caught my attention.

Finally, I was at a school that had wrestling again! They had a summer program and I was able to join during their "open mat" time where any student could go in and practice with the team. I hadn't wrestled since the one year in sixth grade where I lost every match that I wrestled, but I decided to give it a go. I knew my experience and ability to compete against someone my size would help me be more competitive. There were only a few of us that day and I wrestled with the few other kids that were on the team about my size. While I didn't score any points that day, I was able to maintain my base and not allow anyone to turn me over on my back, which meant that I had developed a solid defense, at least. I spent the summer participating in both summer programs and planned to participate in both sports during the winter season if I made the basketball team.

Sometime late in the summer, I found out that I wouldn't be allowed to play both sports since they were the same season. My guess was, since the school was a large suburban school and there were many kids who wanted to play, they did not allow it. I had to choose. While I think I loved basketball more, I was more fitted to be competitive at wrestling so I chose it.

School started that fall and I loved attending Northglenn. It was a large school and there were many opportunities. Even better, the campus was open. At lunch time, we could leave campus and go to McDonalds, Taco Bell or whatever fast food fare was nearby. I suppose that was a time when you could go to the smoker's circle on campus, as well.

One day, I left campus at lunch with some friends to go to McDonald's. We walked the block and a half to the corner and then took a right. McDonald's was another half block down on the opposite side of the street. The street had three lanes on each side with a twelve inch tall concrete barrier between them. After we walked down the half-block, we needed to cross the six lanes of the street. Cars were coming and my friends decided that after a couple of cars sped by, they would take off before the following ones arrived. They darted across the street. I wasn't as confident, so after those initial cars passed by, I paused in the first lane of traffic since the next car coming was in the second lane. That car slowed down for me to go, but I felt it safer to let it go so I waved it on.

Suddenly the car sputtered and died right in the middle of the street. While it did eventually roll past me, the driver could not get it restarted so I darted behind the car as it rolled by and ran over to McDonald's. Apparently, a police officer observed the incident and met me at McDonald's where he gifted me with a jaywalking ticket. To this day, I have never heard of anyone else ever getting a jaywalking ticket, but I did, at fifteen years old. I was both ashamed and dumbfounded, particularly since the entire incident took place because *I let the car go first* instead of darting in front of it. My friends were never even ticketed, though they did the same thing *without* waiting for the car.

The cost of the ticket was fifteen dollars, but my allowance once a month was only six dollars so I knew I couldn't afford it and decided to ignore it. One lucky Sunday morning a few weeks later, we were greeted by a policeman knocking on the door. I wondered what my dad did and why they were there when suddenly it hit me. I hadn't paid my ticket. *Surely they didn't come to my house for that,* I thought. **Surely, they did.** Not only did they come to my house for that, but they literally cuffed me, put me in their car without my parents and booked me at their police station. When we arrived, they fingerprinted me near the holding cells and I thought I was going to prison for not paying a jaywalking ticket that I couldn't afford.

Luckily, my parents arrived within an hour and paid my bail which was over fifty dollars. I knew that I would end up having to pay them back. I also knew that I was dead when we got home. I wasn't sure which was worse. *Should I just go to prison or go home with my dad*, I wondered. Later, after we got home, I had another one of those wonderful experiences with the broom, lots of crying and wishing that I had never lived with that man. All because I got a jaywalking ticket and failed to pay it.

Once November rolled around, wrestling season began and I called it quits on my basketball career. I had never worked out so hard. We lifted. We ran. We wrestled. I really fell in love with the sport and became very competitive. Our team was very large in terms of wrestling teams. We had nearly fifty guys on the team. Many wrestling teams don't cut wrestlers because they want everyone to continue to get experience and make each other better. Only one guy could be varsity at each weight though, so we wrestled against the other guys in our weight class weekly to determine who was varsity. While I never won the varsity spot that year as a sophomore, I was fairly competitive and came close a few times.

I was able to gain a lot of experience though because we participated in many junior varsity matches and tournaments. Oftentimes, wrestling programs don't even attend junior varsity events due to not having many junior varsity wrestlers, but since our team was large we both hosted and attended many of these events. I gained a lot of experience through practice and through these events and I was proud of myself at the end of the season when I finished with fourteen wins and only thirteen losses. I had a winning record as a junior varsity wrestler at a large suburban high school where many of the wrestlers had years of experience over me! I had finally found my sport!

That is until the end of the season, or rather just before. One day when I came home from practice, Dad dropped the bomb on us. We were moving again; back out near Terri and Gary who lived in Deer Trail. Dad missed being closer to Terri and his grandson, Dillian. Though I enjoyed being with Terri and her family, It didn't matter to me. They lived close enough. I finally found wrestling again and did not want to lose it. I was loving being in the city and having all of the opportunities at this large school. I hated living in small towns. I knew I had a chance to be varsity the following year and was excited about my future in wrestling. I was able to talk Dad into staying for a few more weeks to finish the wrestling season and thankfully, he obliged for once.

I won my last wrestling match of the season, which was such a gratifying feeling. That match is what put me over .500 for the season and gave me a winning record at 14-13. I knew I was done at Northglenn and at least had that to hang my hat on. I found out that we weren't moving back to Agate again, though. This time we were moving twelve miles closer to Denver from Deer Trail. I didn't know much about Byers, but I would quickly learn that it wasn't all bad. Byers had a wrestling program and though it was a small town, it was an excellent program. I had hope, once again. The next couple of years changed my life and gave me a platform to launch myself into becoming a man.

Chapter 18

Byers, Colorado Pt 1 (1989)

Though Byers was another small town along the I-70 corridor on the eastern plains of Colorado, Mom's drive was still just under an hour again. We lived on the outskirts of town on a lane in a portion of the trailer park that was nearly abandoned. The trailer park itself was full for three streets with trailers on both sides filling most lots. However, we lived on the fourth street that went in the opposite direction off the county road and only three trailers remained on this street. Each of these remaining trailers were nearly four hundred feet or more apart and on opposite sides of the street from each other. Dead grass and hay fields surrounded the trailers on all sides. Only a few trees were in the area with one providing shade to our house just outside of the driveway. The dirt street that led to our trailer was full of dust, rocks and potholes.

Dad's record collection had continued to grow and was now up to about twelve thousand albums. When we walked into our trailer, up the old rickety wooden steps, we entered into the living room. It was immediately sectioned off with an old buffet and our large TV on a tall table on the right as we entered, creating a hallway into the dining room around the corner on the left. At night Mom and Dad attached a sheet to these two items and the living room was completely closed off since they slept on the sleeper couch. Dad had built his record cabinet mostly on the far wall in the living room and placed his desk in the far corner where you could only see him if you were at just the right angle in the room. He closed off a doorway between the kitchen and his desk so that he could have privacy and use the entire space for his desk area which now consisted of twenty six binders as his record books and everything he needed to maintain the organization of his collection. He also housed multiple stereos in the area, connected to his audio tape decks.

Dad had a separate stereo that was a floor model housed in a glass paneled case that he only used for "presentations" when people came over. His speakers that hooked up to it were a good three to four foot tall and eighteen inches wide. They were on grand display in the living room. When we entered the trailer and went through the makeshift hallway, we turned left into the dining room which contained our pool table. We covered the pool table with two half-sheets of plywood and then covered those with table cloths so that we could also use it as a dinner table. The walls in this room were covered with album covers of both rock and roll and country western artists. The more controversial the album cover, the better and more prominent location it held in the room. Album covers also covered the ceiling, completely *papering* the entire room.

Just behind the pool table was the back door that I had often launched myself out of, to escape my dad. My car was parked behind the trailer on the driveway pad that used to be used for the next trailer when there had been one, so I often used this door anyway. To the right of that door was the kitchen that had previously connected into the living room, but Dad had blocked that off. At the other end of the pool/dining room on the left was an entry way into the first bathroom with a bedroom on each side of the entryway. Shelby's room was on the left and my room was on the right. If we were to walk straight ahead instead of turning left to our rooms, the boys' (all three of them) room was in front of you and the washer and dryer were in their own closet on the right before entering their room. Mom and Dad's bathroom was on the other end of the boys room on their left, though Mom and I were mostly the only ones to use it.

For a trailer, it was pretty decent size which was what we needed since there were seven of us living there. Us kids continued to keep it as clean as we could. My primary job was making dinner, doing the dishes and keeping the kitchen clean. Shelby had the laundry and the bathrooms. Shannon, Jesse and Jason had to keep their room clean and help with the living room and dining room. Mom continued to work at her insurance company, paying claims while Dad worked at his desk, organizing his music and collecting records. He still couldn't work due to his injury and turned his music into his day job, even though it didn't make him any money. He also stayed busy yelling at us to do our chores.

Soon after I started school, I made friends almost immediately with Kent. He lived in our trailer court at the end of one of the full lanes of trailers. He was a bit of a simple guy, but he was nice and invited me into friendship immediately. He lived with his dad and younger brother and wasn't left with much responsibility so we ran and played together as much as we could at fifteen. Kent invited me into friendship with him and his two other friends; Steve and Brian. Steve was a lot of fun and we hung out just a little bit that spring before he moved back to Ohio to live with his dad. Brian mostly hung out and dreamed about being a drummer. He practiced like crazy in his basement on his own set and was quite talented. This was the beginning of what we called, "The Brotherhood."

The four of us became inseparable, except by girls. They divided us no matter how much we decided girls would never come between us. Kent and I ran around more like younger kids on our bikes. We often hung out with younger kids in the trailer court, as well. When Steve, Kent and I hung out, we often played basketball together. When the four of us hung out, we all felt better about ourselves athletically because Brian was the unathletic, band nerd type. But he also lifted weights and was probably stronger than all of us. Brian was so proud of his hair and tanned image since he loved to use a tanning bed.

Byers was a small school compared to Northglenn, but was much larger than Agate. I had twenty-three students in my class at Byers and they offered many more school sport options.

The first and most important sport was wrestling. When we first arrived in Byers, the wrestling season was still going on. Many of their varsity wrestlers had advanced beyond the district tournament. While my season in Northglenn had finished, six out of eight Byers wrestlers also advanced beyond their region to the Colorado State Wrestling Tournament. While I hadn't met them yet, this gave me a lot of hope for wrestling in Byers. *They must be pretty good if that many guys advanced to state*, I thought.

That spring, I participated in track and ran the one and two-mile races in order to stay in shape for wrestling. Track also had two additional benefits; meeting girls and hanging out with Steve and Kent, who also ran track. I wasn't great at track, though I was somewhat competitive, but it didn't matter to me due to the additional benefits.

School in Byers was a fairly positive experience even if I did find myself getting in trouble from time to time. This was the time of my life where much of my shyness came to an end and I became much more social, even turning into a bit of a class clown at times. I had so much fun at Byers High School, feeling free to express who I hoped to be as an athlete and the class clown type. I was still a bit shy with the girls, but Steve, though a year younger than me, showed me the ropes in that area and mentored me.

This is also the time where I developed the "little guy" mindset – Little Guy, Big Mouth. I often ran my mouth to kids I thought were my enemy or against me in some way. I didn't take crap from anyone, anymore. I finally developed confidence from wrestling and since we started to stay in one place a bit longer, I started to develop *longer* term friendships. Steve helped a lot with my confidence, as well, because he was a very confident guy.

"Why don't you go out and find a job?" my dad asked. I had been sitting around the house for a couple of weeks doing nothing but watching TV after school got out for the summer.

"Where would I go? I don't know who's hiring," I responded.

"Just walk through town and stop in all of the businesses and ask if they are hiring and if you can fill out an application," he explained.

I felt stupid thinking about doing such a thing, like my twelve year old self, going to our new neighbors and introducing myself like I did in Bailey.

"Gas stations, grocery stores, banks, restaurants, any place might hire, even if only for the summer," he continued to explain.

I wasn't going to turn sixteen until later in the summer, but I was hoping someone would hire me before my birthday. I wanted to make money to buy a car. I was insistent on getting my license as soon as I could. My parents let me get my permit in January while we still lived in Thornton and I planned to do everything I could to get my license on my sixteenth birthday.

"I guess," I replied sheepishly. I was still pretty shy with adults and walking into their world of work to ask to join it was extremely intimidating. I didn't really know what to say or how to dress. I was unsure who would hire a fifteen year old kid. *Do banks do that?* I wondered. I didn't want to even try to work at a gas station. That was too dirty for me.

I walked out of the back door of our trailer from the dining room where the pool table was situated, stepped onto the back porch and hopped over the fence. I walked down the street several hundred feet passing the only trailer on the opposite side of the street between our trailer and the county road. As I walked down the first lane in the trailer park, I stopped at Kent's trailer, and knocked on the door.

"What's up man?!" Kent asked as he answered the door. He yawned rather largely and stretched his arms.

"I don't know... I think I'm going into town to look for a job," I answered. "What are you up to?"

"I'm just laying around watching TV and my brother."

"Oh," I said, "so you can't go with me because of him?"

"No, I better not," he explained. "My dad will kick my butt if I leave him alone and we definitely can't take him with us! Where you going?"

"Not sure... just thought I would walk through town, stop in and ask. I'm definitely going to the grocery and the two restaurants."

"Well, good luck!" he said "I'm chillin'." Kent went back to watching TV and I took the path at the end of their street to the right. The path led past the other trailer park streets and I hopped the fence at the end to take the shortcut past the gas station. Across the street from the gas station was the local bank and the Byers General Store. I walked in the bank nervously looking around. I spotted an open teller and walked up to her.

"Are you taking applications?" I asked. She smiled generously and lightly laughed.

"No, sweetie. You have to be eighteen to work here."

"I figured," I said, "just thought I would ask." I walked out feeling like an idiot and knew I would never find a job. I walked up the parking lot to the grocery store. I stepped on the rubber pad outside the store and the door automatically opened. The smell of fresh produce and small town grocery filled my senses as I walked in. *This could be it. I could see myself working here*, I thought. *That would be nice.* I walked around the store for a while, looking around as if a job was going to greet me somewhere in the aisles. After walking around for a bit, I nervously asked an employee stacking tuna cans, "where can I apply for a job?"

"Oh, I don't think we are hiring," he answered. "But you can go to the customer service desk to get an application if you want."

"Thank you, sir," I responded, hoping my politeness would count for something if that guy had a say in hiring me. I walked to the front of the store and looked around for the customer service desk. A cashier directed me to the end of the cash registers. I walked over and rang the bell. Suddenly, someone popped up from behind the counter.

"Sorry, didn't see you there," she said as she looked down on me from the tall counter. "How can I help you?"

"I was wondering if you were hiring. Can I fill out an application?"

"Oh, no. We're not hiring right now. You can try back later in a few weeks. Are you sixteen yet?" she asked.

"No, not yet. I'll be sixteen next month," I explained.

"Well, maybe come back then. You have to be sixteen to work here."

"Ok, thank you." I said feeling about as dumb as a kid could. I walked up the street toward the highway past our small town hotel that set right off the highway. I walked under the overpass of the highway and continued toward the main part of our small town. There were no sidewalks, only blacktop and dirt paths. My next stop was the Golden Spike Inn.

The Golden Spike Inn was a restaurant on one side of the building and a bar on the other side. The two sides were connected by a hallway in the front where the bathrooms were located. I walked in the front door and wondered if I should go left into the restaurant or right into the bar. *Was the restaurant even open?* I wondered since I didn't notice many cars out front. I decided to play it safe and took a left into the restaurant. Thankfully, it was open. I walked around the corner and took a right to where the cash register was situated. The restaurant was empty of customers, but I could hear sounds in the kitchen area behind the cash register, though I couldn't see anyone yet.

"Hello?" I said, looking around to see if I was missing something.

"Oh, hi!" came a friendly voice from the waitress station back and to the right from the register. An older lady came out and smiled at me. "How can I help you?" she asked.

"I was just wondering if you were hiring?" I asked.

"Oh, great!" she said. "We need a dishwasher!" She was sweet and kind, also very happy and joyous. "Follow me," she instructed and walked into the kitchen. I followed her into the kitchen, not knowing what I was getting into. The dishwashing station was immediately on the right and the cooking area was immediately on the left with a food serving station between the cooking area and where we walked in. She led me past both of these areas, to the right, into an office.

"Here you go," she said. "Fill this out." She handed me an application. "How old are you?" she asked. I was afraid to answer, knowing what was liable to happen next, but I did anyway.

"I'm only fifteen, but I'll be sixteen next month."

"Oh, that's fine," she said. "We can get you started right now, if you want?"

I was so relieved. It sounded like I already had the job. *This seemed easy*, I thought. It was less than a half-hour before that I thought I would never get a job.

I started the job the following day washing dishes for the Golden Spike Inn. The restaurant was a small town steakhouse that served food in both the restaurant and the bar. After working there for the summer as a dishwasher, I started learning the ropes on the cooking side and quickly became an assistant prep cook. It wasn't long before I could cook a few items all by myself when the cook left early on any given night. The bar served food after the restaurant closed, so I was called on often to fill the bill.

I was able to make some decent money that summer and saved it to buy a car. My parents had bought a 1976 Chevy Ventura for themselves as one of their cars. It got terrible gas mileage and had a loud glasspack muffler (designed to be extra loud).

One day, near my birthday when my dad knew I was going to be getting my license soon, he offered to let me buy it from them for the same price they paid for it, $250. I quickly and excitedly agreed. I had enough money and now I would have my own car!

Finally, my birthday arrived and since it fell on a Saturday, my mom could take me to get my license. I was thankful for that because even though my dad taught me how to drive, I was much less nervous driving with Mom. There were two places that I knew I could take the test. I could go into Denver or out to a small town outside Limon called Hugo. Hugo was an even smaller dirt town and I heard from many others that passing their test was much easier, so I decided to go there. I studied hard for my test and was well prepared for the big day!

On the morning of my birthday, we arrived at the driver's license bureau. To my delight and excitement, I didn't even have to wait. There was an evaluator available. We signed up, filled out the paperwork, showed proof of insurance (which we kept for a couple of days just to get my license) and then I took the written exam. I felt confident since I had prepared well. After the test, the evaluator invited me outside to our vehicle and jumped in the car with me.

"Don't worry about anything, just do your best. I'll be writing notes whether you do it right or wrong, so don't worry about me," she said nicely. That was a relief. I was definitely nervous, but I knew I could do well in this small town. I pulled out of the parking lot being sure to move slowly, use my mirrors, turn signals and be extra cautious. We drove a pretty large circle through town, stopping at a few stop signs, passing the local hospital, and then onto the street that turned into a county road. Finally, we completed the large circle and arrived back at the parking lot. I felt confident. I did well.

"Very good," she said. "I was impressed, for such a young driver, you did well. You used your turn signals well. I only had two areas I would give you feedback on." *Oh gosh,* I thought, *what did I mess up?*

"When we drove by the hospital, I didn't see you use your mirrors or pay close enough attention to your surroundings. There weren't any issues to fail you there, but you need to pay closer attention in a hospital zone." I was nervous, but happy she wasn't going to fail me.

"However, shortly after we first left the parking lot, you drove right through a stop sign without even slowing down," she continued. My mind began racing. *What? I don't remember any stop sign that I ran. I was super careful looking out for everything,* I thought.

"What?" I asked. "When was that? I don't remember missing or running any stop sign!" I said with a bit of nervous franticness in my voice.

"That first block after we took a right out of the parking lot. There is a stop sign on a small tree. I don't think you even saw it." My mind raced. *No!!!! I don't remember that,* I thought. "Unfortunately, that would have resulted in a moving violation and for that I have to fail you." I thought my life was coming to an end.

"You can try again on our next business day, which is Monday." My head dropped. Mom had to work on Monday. Dad would have to bring me and I didn't even know if he would. I went home that day sad and depressed because I didn't get my license on my birthday, wondering if I ever would. But before we went home, we drove by that *invisible* stop sign that I missed.

"There it is," my mom said and pointed in front of the car to the right. She was right. The stop sign was posted, not on a metal pole though. It was posted on a small tree. *How could I have missed that?* I thought. I didn't remember seeing it at all.

Thankfully, Dad did bring me back on Monday. I stopped at the stop sign during my test, paid extra close attention to my mirrors and surroundings in the hospital zone and passed with flying colors. Dad didn't even make me nervous and I became a licensed driver! Afterwards, Dad even took me to Rip Griffin's Truck Stop in Limon to celebrate by eating "All-You-Can-Eat Steak" for $8.99.

A little over a week later, at the beginning of August, I started my first real bout with tackle football. Byers played eight-man tackle football. Since I didn't really watch football on TV yet and I had only played six-man flag football or street football with friends, I was very unfamiliar with what seemed like a whole new sport. But I knew football would be great preparation for my wrestling season. *It would get me in shape and make me more aggressive,* I thought. So I played tackle football for the first time. I learned a lot. I did get in great shape. But I still didn't play much. I was still pretty small at only one hundred and twenty pounds and five foot, four inches tall.

I felt like I never really got a fair chance as I watched some of the freshmen on the team pass me by for playing time even though they weren't much bigger. Nobody on the team worked harder than me and I was always cheering my teammates on from the sidelines. Never-the-less, I was glad to practice, get in great shape and was better prepared for my real season – wrestling! That was my first taste at real athletic success.

Chapter 19

Byers, Colorado Pt 2 (1989)

"Ricky was a young boy. He had a heart of stone. Lived nine to five and he worked his fingers to the bone," sang *Skid Row* through my headphones connected to my Sony Walkman. The sound of jump ropes and fans yelling in the stands filled the gym. I was busy staying warm and getting psyched up behind the bleachers by jumping rope and listening to my latest favorite band. There were just a few more matches in the heavyweight rounds taking place to determine who would be in the finals. The gym smelled of sweat and hope as everyone watched in anticipation.

I spent the afternoon wrestling my way through my first varsity tournament after getting a bye in the first round and then winning my next two matches – both pins. I was filled with excitement, and fear, since I knew my best competition was coming up. Ty Freel wrestled for our rival school from the next town over and had developed quite the reputation already. People called him dangerous and nasty. He had this great finishing move that was called by some – a headlock, but by the wrestling community – a head and arm. His first two matches, after his first round bye, resulted in first period pins with the head and arm.

I had paid close attention since I was warned by some of my teammates that he was probably the best wrestler at my weight and had earned the number one seed. His head and arm were deadly, they said. In his first match he wrestled, he smacked the other kid around a bit at the beginning causing the wrestler to get frustrated and annoyed enough to let his guard down. Once the other wrestler let his guard down, Ty took his right hand that grasped the back of his opponents head as they faced each other, then slid his hand and arm around the head completely where he grabbed the deltoid of his unsuspecting opponent. At the same time, he rotated his hips around in a counter-clockwise motion sinking them deep inside of his opponent's space causing his body to slide over his hips and on his side. The other wrestler's feet immediately left the mat as Ty pulled him over the top and raised his right elbow high, throwing his opponent's shoulder blades straight to the mat. Ty immediately pulled up on the arm that stayed in the air and his opponent's head, sitting his butt out as far as he could.

The look of determination and arrogant pride showed on his face as he smiled, knowing his win was imminent. Not two or three seconds went by when the referee that had been on his feet quickly followed the action to the mat, sliding down on his own side and rotating his head around so that he could view the opponent's shoulder blades now firmly pressed against the mat. *SMACK!* came the sound as the referee hit the mat with his open hand. Ty wrenched on his opponent's head one more time for good measure before letting go and jumped to his feet.

That same smile of pride and disgust of his clearly inferior opponent resonated on his face at the same time. He lifted both hands up and then punched his right fist into the air, while circling around to the center of the mat where he met his opponent once again. They shook hands and the referee grabbed Ty's hand and stretched it high into the air indicating he was the winner.

I watched again a few hours later when the same match repeated itself almost identically with a different opponent. While I had pinned both of my opponents that day, the first was quicker and I had used a typical, basic single leg takedown followed by a half-nelson pin in the first period. My second match was a bit more challenging as we went three periods, but I was finally able to get the pin with that same basic half-nelson. My mind replayed Ty's matches over and over as I listened to Skid Row belt out their latest album through my headphones. *He's not gonna put me in a head and arm,* I told myself. I watched his set up and knew not to get too close or to press back knowing that he would try and catch me off guard while I was focused on the wrong things before he would throw me off my feet.

"Let's go!" Luke yelled as he smacked me on the shoulder. Luke, our one hundred and forty pound wrestler notified me that it was time to line up for the finals. While I had heard about the finals line up, I had never participated in it and wasn't really sure what it was. I followed Luke up to the mat on the far side of the gym. "Get in line by weight," he explained. I noticed that the line on our side of the mat was already forming with the smaller wrestlers, beginning with the one hundred and three pound wrestlers. I jumped in the third spot in line as our one hundred and nineteen pound wrestler. I noticed that we had six wrestlers in the finals and I smiled. Finally, I had arrived in a sport. I was wrestling in my first varsity wrestling tournament and had made the finals. Our team had six wrestlers out of the thirteen weight classes in the finals. We were dominating. The lights in the gym suddenly went out and "Eye of the Tiger" by Survivor came over the loudspeakers and a low hush came over the crowd as everyone quieted down.

"Welcome to the Brush Wrestling Tournament Finals!" the announcer said loudly. A spotlight danced around the room and then settled on the center circle in the middle. "Wrestling in the finals at one hundred and three pounds," the announcer continued. He announced each weight and when he arrived at my weight, "from Byers, Shawn Conjeltun." I died inside. *Will they ever get my name right?* I wondered. I was annoyed, but I was also pumped about my opportunity and early success. I wished my parents were there to see it. Brush was over an hour and a half away and while we had been there all day, I only wrestled a total of about seven minutes to that point. Many parents didn't come, but I really appreciated my friend's parents that did come and brought snacks to share with the team throughout the day.

The line-up announcements continued as opponents met in the center circle in the middle of the mat to shake hands as they called both names. When I shook Ty's hand, I knew I could beat him. He had one move. No way I would let him use it on me. Finally, the announcements came to an end. The wrestlers all went to their desired warm up spot and waited their turn as the one hundred and three pounders made it to the center mat first. They always started at the smaller weights and worked their way up. I knew I was third and would be up soon, so I went back behind the bleachers to jump rope and listen to my psych-me-up music. I rewound the tape to Skid Row's "18 and Life" and pressed play. The jump rope swirled around my head over and over. I was ready.

When I heard them announce the beginning of the one hundred and twelve pound match, I made my way matside, near the corner where I met my coach.

"You ready?" he asked, smiling. Coach was an old wrestler himself, as most wrestling coaches are. He had those great coaching shorts from the eighties that make their way up to mid-stomach. He wore his Byers High School polo tucked into them tightly with no overhang. He was a fairly large man at about five foot eleven and two hundred and thirty pounds or so. He wore these deep coke bottle glasses that looked like they had a permanent shadow attached. He was a solid guy and a solid coach. I felt like he really cared even though he didn't get too personal. He just smiled a lot and said some positive things once in a while. He had been here before, but this was all new to me.

"Yeah, coach. Ready as I'll ever be!" I responded. I was pumped. My pre-match routine had me psyched as I envisioned Ty trying to set up his head and arm, squirming out and hitting a single leg, leaving him baffled. As I took him to the mat in my mind, I quickly moved into turning him to his back and throwing in my finishing half-nelson. Suddenly, I noticed the one hundred and twelve pound match just ended after all three periods with a score of 7-4. *The finals are a tough place*, I thought. *Both guys are great wrestlers, otherwise they wouldn't be in the finals. Maybe my match will go the distance*, I wondered. I just hoped I would come out on top.

"Let's go!" coach yelled and slapped me on the butt. I quickly removed my wrestling warm up pants and my favorite Bart Simpson t-shirt that I used as a warm up top. I pulled the strap from the left side of my head gear that sat loosely on my head over to the right side across the bottom of my chin and buckled it tight. I smacked both sides of my head gear as if to test its strength and durability. I was ready to go and I bounded into the center of the circle. I could hear "18 and Life" playing in my mind as I envisioned how the match would go. I placed my toe on the starting line on my side of the center circle. Ty did the same on his side. I was ready. He was ready. We quickly shook hands and let go.

"Whhhrrrr," the whistle sounded, starting the match. We began circling around the center, while darting our hands toward each other and back to our sides, feeling each other out trying to get a sense of quickness and style. Suddenly, he reached up and grabbed the back of my head and pulled down as if he was trying to slam my head straight to the mat. Of course, I didn't allow it and I pulled back. I was careful not to expose myself so that he didn't take advantage of me as I was pulling back. *That ain't happenin',* I thought. *He's not going to muscle me around or toy with me,* my mind continued.

I reached up and grabbed the back of his head and we both engaged in a similar hold as if to test the other's strength, pushing and pulling to see where one of us might gain an advantage. I didn't let go right away, like he did. I held on and continued to try and steer him around by yanking and moving my feet to declare my dominance.

After about ten to fifteen seconds of this, the ref yelled at us, "move it back to the center!" I noticed we had moved near the edge of the mat and decided to heed the referee's command. I let up and moved back to the center of the mat while facing my opponent. We both danced back to the center, facing each other, weighing our distance and readiness to make a move at any moment. We moved our hands back and forth again as if to get a better gauge and see if we could get the other guy to flinch long enough to make a move. Neither of us did, so we grabbed each other behind the head and started to tussle again near the center of the mat this time. I pulled down, hoping he would pull back and expose himself to a single-leg take-down. No luck as he pulled back in a very measured way. He was stronger than I had anticipated.

He pulled down on me trying to do the same and I was already getting tired after warming up for quite some time before the match. I imagine I had already expended so much energy just psyching myself up and jumping rope, but we were early in the match and I wasn't that tired yet. I quickly took a shot toward his legs, but it was half-hearted since I hadn't really set it up. He barely had to jump back to dismiss it. *I have to get closer,* I thought. *We are way too far away for my single-leg shot.* I decided to move in and ready myself for the shot. As I stepped in and grabbed the back of his head, he grabbed the back of my head. I was just about ready to shuck his head aside and I rose up for just a second. As I did, he made his move.

Suddenly, the last two matches that I watched Ty wrestle that day played over in my mind as I began to relive it in real time. Ty took his right hand that grasped the back of my head as we faced each other. He slid it around my head completely and grabbed my deltoid as I was now the next unsuspecting opponent. At the same time, he rotated his hips around in a counter-clockwise motion sinking them deep inside of my space causing my body to slide over his hips and on his side. My feet immediately left the mat as he pulled me over the top and raised his right elbow high throwing my shoulder blades straight to the mat. Ty immediately pulled up on my arm and head, sitting his butt out as far as he could.

SMACK! came the sound as the referee hit the mat. *What the?!* I thought as I laid there dumbfounded. I had been pinned. I lost! I had been stuck in a head and arm after I knew exactly what he wanted to do. *How the heck did that just happen?* I asked myself. That was the one thing I wasn't going to let happen and yet, it did. I was confused, sad and angry! Ty had let go of me and bounced to his feet, smiling with the same happy and proud smug look that he had earlier in the day. I jumped to my feet and walked to the center of the circle. The ref pulled our hands together and we quickly shook. We let go and I looked at him with disgust. I turned my head and walked away.

As I turned, I saw my coach who had this "well you tried" look on his face. Then he pointed me toward the opposite side of the mat. "Go shake the coach's hand," he directed. In my frustration and confusion, I had forgotten to shake his coach's hand. I turned around, returned to the other side of the mat where I shook the coach's hand. I couldn't tell you what he looked like. I was so disgusted with myself.

Later, on the long bus ride home, I realized that I still earned second place after winning two matches and that was quite an accomplishment for me. Pride started to fill my heart and I was happy to have found my sport. I had a chance to be really good. I set a goal in my mind to work hard and I knew I would get another chance to wrestle Ty. After all, he was at our rival school, only six miles away.

That night when I got home at nearly ten o'clock Mom, Dad, Gary, Terri and a friend of Gary's were still up playing pool and drinking. The house was filled with cigarette smoke and the smell of cheap booze. There was laughter and a light, fun mood. Shelby and Shannon were hanging out too, even though they were only eleven and eight respectively. Music was boomin' on the stereo and they were having a good time.

"There he is!" Dad said when I walked around the corner from the front door and entered the pool room. "Shawn's been wrestling all day. You ready to play some pool, Shawn?" Dad asked.

"I'm always ready," I said confidently. "Are you ready?" I asked in a cocky way.

"Ma, write it up. I got Terri, you and Shawn, Gary and Jim," he said. Mom walked over to the chalkboard which hung on top of the album covers we used as wallpaper. She wrote up three columns and set up a scoring system.

Well, this seems like fun, I thought. I loved playing pool when it got competitive. I could tell that Shelby and Shannon had been allowed to play before I got home, but now they were told to go to bed. I got to play with the big boys. I was emotionally confused though. I had been really excited about the wrestling tournament, making the finals and winning two matches. I was frustrated and discouraged from losing in the finals the way I did. Dad didn't even ask how it went. We never discussed it. I didn't know how to talk about it anyway, and was probably a little relieved that I didn't have to.

We played pool for three or four hours while they all drank and Dad played his mix-tapes that he spent all day creating. They listened mostly to country music since that is what Gary and Jim liked. *We lived in "Hickville, USA" and it was most appropriate anyway,* I thought. I hated country music, but it was home. My pool playing didn't mind it though as Mom and I were racking up the wins.

After about three hours, Mom and I had won twelve games, Dad and Terri had won eight, and Gary and Jim won five. We were on a roll. I didn't know if that was because we were the least drunk or we really were the better players. Dad had always been the best individual player, but he usually picked the worst player to counter-balance that a little. He liked to keep it competitive rather than dominate. That night, we came out on top. Until the end of the night.

As I knocked the eight ball into the corner pocket and looked at their three balls left on the table, I smiled as smugly as Ty Freel ever did right at my dad. Suddenly, my dad's countenance changed. He had been smiling, but then he stopped.

"You think your hot sh*t?!" Dad said.

"Tonight, I am," I replied, continuing to smile, but now wondered if I should.

"You ain't sh*t!" he said. "Let's go, just you and me. One game, for ten dollars." he said.

"No," I said. "I don't like to play for money. I don't have much since I can't work as much during wrestling season," I explained.

"You think your hot sh*t, put your money where your mouth is. Ten dollars, rack em up!" he ordered. I shook my head, but realized it didn't matter. We were going to play the game either way. I went over to the rack and set the balls up for him to break. "Go ahead," he said, "you can break." I returned to the other end of the table and lined up the cue ball. Everyone else was just watching, not really sure what to say.

"I think we're out of here," Gary said and motioned for Jim and Terri to head out.

"No, just wait," Dad said. "I want you to see me kick his *ss." Gary laughed and Jim snickered. I pulled back the cue stick and blasted away hoping to see balls go everywhere. It was a solid break, but the center balls didn't move much. Other balls went all over the table, but nothing fell in.

"Thanks, Shawn," Dad said. "Just the way I like it. All bust, no balls." Dad hobbled over to the table and began to shoot. His leg still wasn't great since the accident, but when he had been drinking, it got even worse. He almost stumbled to the floor a couple of times, but he maintained his balance by holding on to the table. One after the other he began to sink ball after ball. His fun, light hearted demeanor disappeared. He became focused and calculated as each and every shot went exactly how he wanted and left him set for his next shot. I sat there and watched. I knew he was going to be on his game now since I acted like I was big stuff. I knew I wouldn't have many shots so I would have to take advantage of what I did have.

When it was my turn, I went to the table and took aim. Most of the table was clear now that he had made most of his shots. I made my first one that was pretty easy and already close to the pocket. As I aimed down on my second shot, I thought about how I would need to leave myself set for the following shot which caused me to miss slightly on that shot. I was nervous. He was about to wipe me off the table. Dad returned and knocked down his last two balls. He was now on the eight ball and I still had six balls left on the table.

"Down in the corner," he said as he pointed to the other end of the table. He pulled back as smooth as I ever saw him play and in a calculated shot, he drove the cue ball into the eight ball which cut sharply down and into the corner pocket ever so on target. *Crap*, I thought, *so much for being big stuff.* Dad was still Dad. I was put back in my place. "Put the money on the table," Dad said.

"I'll get it tomorrow," I said. "I'm tired and going to bed."

"Bullsh*t. Put the money on the table right now. You play for money, you do it right. Put the money on the table," he ordered as he smirked at me.

"Okay, let me go get it from my room," I said sheepishly. I walked back to my room and opened the door. My room was a mess. I hoped I could find it. I really wasn't sure where it was or if I even had it for sure. It had been a long day and I had worked the night before. That reminded me that I had collected my pay, which was in cash and put it in my top drawer. I reached in, grabbed it and returned to the pool room.

"Here you go," I said as I laid two five dollar bills on the table.

"When you get big enough to beat me for money, then you can talk sh*t," my dad said looking at me intensely and serious. I backed up to the other side of the table not knowing what to expect. "Ma, let's go to bed," he ordered, now to Mom. Gary, Jim and Terri said their goodbyes and walked out the front door. They had twelve miles to drive back to Deer Trail where they lived. Terri had the least to drink and probably drove home, I hoped.

As soon as the front door closed, Dad continued, "Shawn! Get that f*cking kitchen cleaned up before you go to bed. It looks like sh*t." I kinda smiled and laughed sarcastically. *He* *was just upset that he got beat playing teams and now he's taking it out on me,* I thought.

"Something funny, you little piece of sh*t?!" Dad asked, yelling at me. I was still on the other side of the table and was now starting to realize this might get physical so I stayed on the opposite side of the table from him.

"No. I wasn't here tonight to do it. I was hoping to do it in the morning," I pleaded, but started to realize I should have just done it.

"You get that f*cking kitchen clean and you do it right now!" he screamed. Dad was in full fury at this point. He started toward me from the opposite side of the table, but began to stumble and caught himself using the table as a crutch. As he stumbled toward me on the right side of the table, I moved toward the left side keeping the table centered between us as if Ty and I were still in the center circle. There was no way I was going to let him get to me. As he stumbled again, he reached out on the pool table and grabbed a ball off the table. I was afraid he was going to throw it at me, so as I stepped again to center the table between us, I got lower in my base as if I was going to wrestle the table, readying myself to duck under it.

"Okay," I said. "I'll do it right now," I pleaded hoping that would make him happy and he would just drop it and go to bed.

"Ma! Let's go to bed," he said, directing her to assist him to the living room, knowing they would have to walk right by me to get there.

I was convinced, though, that he was finally going to bed and would let it rest. As he came by me, he reached out and grabbed me by my t-shirt collar. My dad was about two hundred and twenty pounds at this time and I had just wrestled at one hundred and nineteen pounds that day. He was a much bigger man and I was deathly afraid of him, but as he grabbed me in his drunken state, my wrestling instincts kicked in and I swung him down to the ground at my feet. I quickly steadied my body over the top of his and straddled him as he lay on his back. I grabbed his arms and crossed them in such a way that he couldn't do anything with them. I don't remember pulling a hand back to hit him, but suddenly Mom yelled.

"Don't hit him!" she pleaded.

What? I thought. I was so confused. *Was she telling **me** not to hit **Dad**?*

"I'm not going to hit him!" I yelled. "That's what he does. I'm never going to be like him." I pushed away from him as he lay on his back helpless. I turned and found the back door just a few feet from where we were and bounced out the door. I hopped over the fence and jumped in my car. I had left the keys in the ignition so I started it up, pulled out of the driveway and headed over to Steve's house.

I couldn't believe what I had just heard. After the day that I just had, success in wrestling and pool. I fell short, earning second place twice. My dad's drunken idiocy had led to him treating me like a piece of crap and going after me physically. Then Mom turned and defended him! She never told him to go to bed, to not talk to me that way, to not hit me. No, she told **me** not to hit **him**. That's when I realized I was all alone in my plight.

Thankfully, I had sports to keep my mind and focus. My success in wrestling was just beginning and it kept me focused. It was the one thing that kept me in Byers when Dad was ready to move again.

Chapter 20

Byers, Colorado Pt 3 (1989-1990)

I worked at the Golden Spike Inn as often as possible. One reason is that it kept me out of the house. Another reason was that I wanted to make as much money as possible since I paid for my own gas and bought my own clothes. After I started working, I no longer had chores at home and therefore didn't receive an allowance. My parents would buy me cheap clothes from K-mart or Goodwill, but if I wanted something better, I had to buy it. I enjoyed working and I took pride in what I did. I started as a dishwasher and worked my way up to prep cook. Eventually, I was able to stand in as the primary cook when our only chef was out. I typically worked the afternoons when it was slow and late evening hours until they shut down the service of food in the bar area, which was around 11 p.m.

One day that fall, we got a new waitress. Her name was Cathy. She was closer in age to my parents, but she was a nice, fun lady. She always had a positive attitude and we really enjoyed working together. I appreciated her spirit and she was really impressed by my ability to cook for a restaurant at a young age. One afternoon, she began telling me about her son who lived with his dad in Ohio.

"Hey Shawn!" I could hear what I thought was a southern twang in her voice. "Guess what?! My son is going to move back home!" she said.

"Really?" I asked. "That's great!"

"Yeah, he moved out to Ohio about six months ago. He was just getting to be a handful and needed his dad to put him in his place," she explained.

"What happened? Did he not like that? Is that why he's moving back?" I asked.

"Oh, no. I think they got along okay. He loves his dad. I think he just missed his momma and his sister, Em," she explained. "You know he's only a little younger than you. Byers is a small school. You probably even met him."

"What's his name again?" I asked.

"Steve!" she said, assuming that would mean something to me.

"That's a pretty popular name," I said "Not sure."

"Here, let me see if I have a picture in my purse." She started rummaging through her purse and finally found a small, vinyl wallet insert set of pictures. "Here, Shawn. Look, here's Steve!" she said excitedly as she handed me the pictures.

"Oh my gosh! I do know him! Steve was friends with Kent, Brian and I! He was one of our brothers!" I said. "I can't believe I didn't realize that's who you were talking about."

"Shawn, you're so silly! You knew him all this time?!" I just laughed.

"I can't believe Steve is moving back! Wait until Kent and Brian find out!" I said enthusiastically.

Cathy and I worked together for several months in the evening or on the weekends, but this was her second, or even third job. She was in the Air Force Reserve and regularly drove for about an hour and a half to the base outside Colorado Springs on the weekends. She also had a day job in Denver or somewhere, but I wasn't sure what that was. When she went to it, Steve and I were left in their house with no supervision. That was all I needed to know. Steve moved back a few months later and we reconnected our friendship. Though Steve didn't know much about wrestling, he always gave me props for my success.

I finished out that season of wrestling, not actually winning first place in any tournament, but was still pretty successful with a final record of twenty-three wins and only eleven losses. I was able to place high enough at our district and regional tournaments to advance to the Colorado State Wrestling Tournament.

While the district and regional tournaments were held far away in small podunk towns like Byers, the state tournament was held in Denver at McNichols Arena where the Denver Nuggets played NBA games. The arena was incredible and I was in awe when we walked in for the first time. It was so huge and held about sixteen or seventeen thousand people. The floor space held about ten full-size wrestling mats and they were sectioned off for the different school sizes (A, AA, and AAA). Byers was the smallest school size at the single A size. That didn't matter to me. I had still accomplished quite a feat making it to state that year.

However, my first match pitched me against the predicted state champion at my weight. The weather was terrible and

Mom had promised me that she would come watch me that night after she finished work since she was already in Denver. I didn't really know if she would since she had only come to one tournament that year, which was in Bennett. *She only attended that one because it was on the way home from work one Saturday afternoon,* I reminded myself. Mom worked a lot of Saturdays and Dad never came. The weather was really snowy that Thursday so as the story was told to me, he drove her into work and then was going to drive her home. Due to the situation, they both came to my match that night.

Then came time for my match. I was pitted against Jonah Olguin who had pinned every guy at his regional tournament and all in the first period. I knew what was ahead of me and unlike my uber confidence against Ty Freel, I quickly realized that regardless of any scouting in advance, there probably wasn't much of a chance to win. I was just happy to be there and knew that I was going to wrestle my best. When my time came, I was escorted through the back hallways of McNichols arena where NBA players enter every week. Being behind the scenes of such a great arena was pretty incredible, but then I was led to the floor where the mats lay in the center of the arena. When I stepped out and looked up, I could see ten to fifteen thousand people watching from above.

Time stopped and my heart beat just about as quick as it could. I was overwhelmed with what I was experiencing as I looked around the arena when suddenly I was directed to my mat. My eyes and mind transitioned quickly to the task at hand. *If I can get out the first period, I have a shot at this,* I thought. *Don't get caught in the head and arm,* I thought knowing that was one of his specialties just like Ty.

"Let's go!" coach said loudly and patted me on the back. I dropped my warm up gear, attached my headgear and bounced out to the center of the mat. I looked up in the crowd for a moment wondering if my parents ever actually came, but doubting it. I turned my head to my opponent, set my foot on the line and shook his hand. The whistle sounded off and we both immediately started darting our hands toward one another and circling the center. I made a couple of half-hearted fake shots to see how he would respond, but it was pretty clear he wasn't concerned. Finally, I jabbed my hand toward his head, pulled it back quickly and took a solid shot. He countered, by stepping back, throwing his hand across my face and securing a head and arm. He grabbed me and threw me as hard as he could. My feet went flying in the air and my back smacked on the mat out of bounds.

    The ref blew his whistle and yelled, "out of bounds, no takedown, no backpoints!" I survived his throw and the score was still zero to zero! *I could do this,* I thought. But boy oh boy, was he strong and quick! The rest of the match was a blur. I made it to the second period, but he put me in this move called the spladle. I was left with my butt and private parts facing the large arena crowd and my shoulders were on the mat. I felt like a pretzel and had no idea how I got there. The ref smacked the mat less than thirty seconds into the second period. I had lost, as expected, but I put up a fight. Jonah ended up winning the state championship that year so I didn't feel as bad. I lost my next match in the consolation bracket, but had been proud of myself for making it that far. I now had a vision for how far I could make it and hoped to place my senior year.

    I couldn't believe how far I had come from losing every match that I wrestled in sixth grade to not having a chance to wrestle again for years, floundering in other sports to finally being able to wrestle JV my sophomore year and earning a winning record to making it to state my junior year. I was proud of my accomplishments! As it turned out, Dad did bring Mom to my match that night. That was Dad's only match of mine that he ever watched. I got pinned with my butt in the air and mixed up like a pretzel by the eventual state champ. *But at least he came once*, I told myself.

Spring rolled around and track season arrived. Steve and I both ran track so we hung out a lot more after he returned from Ohio. He taught me how to talk to girls; how to "romanticize" them through love notes and opening doors and such. We figured out ways to follow up those Saturday track afternoons by driving to different local towns to see the girls we met on the Sundays following the meets. When I wasn't able to take my car, Steve would ask his mom if we could take their car. She would only let us if I drove, since Steve didn't have his license. He begged his mom to let him anyway, but she trusted me more regardless. As soon as we left the house and got around the corner though, he would order me to pull over and let him drive. I always did.

One afternoon when we did that on a late Spring day, Steve jumped in the driver's seat. We headed on down the street, took a right and passed over the railroad tracks. As we did, a convertible car drove by that had several teen girls in it. Our heads turned and watched the girls as we tried to figure out if we knew them and how pretty they were. As they looked at us, we waved hoping to garner their attention. It was about this time that Steve was supposed to stop at the stop sign before crossing State Route 40 that went through the center of town. When my head turned around to face the front, I saw a blur on my right.

"Stop!!!" I yelled and pressed my foot to the floor as hard and quick as I could on the passenger side. It wasn't quick enough and there was no break on the passenger side. A large pick up truck barreled into the engine area of the car on my side. Glass went flying everywhere and we wondered if our life was passing before our eyes. The car spun counterclockwise and ended up about a hundred and fifty degrees from the direction it had been facing. Thankfully, neither of us were hurt, but Cathy or "Mom" as I often called her never fully trusted me again. Dad really started to hate Steve now since "he almost killed me," as he said. Of course, Dad never liked anyone for long, so it was a bit expected.

Steve and I had quite a few adventures driving around Byers and to other towns to see girls. We regularly drove around town, sliding around corners and doing all sorts of crazy things. One summer afternoon that year, we found a construction sign that was blinking just lying in the ditch. We picked it up and put it in the backseat of the car and drove around town with it. We took my bb-gun and drove around shooting cats with just one or two pumps. In our technical estimation, this wasn't enough to even break their skin, but it was enough to send them jumping several feet into the air. We flew around town time and time again sliding around corners often times in my parents brand new Hyundai Elantra, pulling the emergency brake to see how far we could slide. It's a wonder we didn't kill anyone, but we had a lot of fun together being crazy teenagers!

One summer afternoon, we drove into the school lot where students park. Our lot was mostly dirt, right off the concrete driveway. We knew no one was at the school since it was summer, so we had our fun doing figure eights and sliding around in the parking lot. Suddenly, another vehicle came around from the other side of the school building and began driving toward us.

"That's Grandstaff's car!" Steve exclaimed.

I immediately realized he was talking about the principal. My heart sunk and I knew we were dead. "Come on, let's get out of here!" he said knowing we couldn't just stay there like sitting ducks. I turned the car and drove directly towards the car coming at us and then right past it. I was afraid to even look and confirm it's driver. I just kept driving, hoping the principal wouldn't know who I was since I was in my parent's car. "Go, go!" Steve said, encouraging me to pick up the speed.

As I turned left out of the parking lot and back toward those train tracks where we had our accident, we noticed the car had turned around and was now following us. "Come on, he's right behind us," Steve said. He was squirming in his seat and had no idea what would happen if we were caught. I continued to drive through town and he followed us everywhere we went.

"I'm gonna get on the highway," I said. "He's not gonna follow us on the highway." I pulled onto Interstate 70 driving east, away from Denver. Sure enough, the car stayed on the town street and did not follow us. We were free! "I just hope he didn't take down our license plate number and report us!" I told Steve.

"I doubt it. I don't think he even knew who we were," Steve said convincingly. "Let's go see if we can find some Strasburg girls," Steve suggested.

"We're headed toward Deer Trail dummy!" I said.

"Well, turn around. There's no girls in Deer Trail. All the hot girls are in Strasburg!" he ordered. We drove another six miles down the interstate, exited the highway and took the state route back through Byers on our way to Strasburg. That's when I realized I hadn't even done anything with my hair. I didn't have the best hair, naturally. I used a lot of product like mousse and gel, though never at the same time. It was absolutely necessary, if we were going to see girls. I checked my hair in the rearview mirror as I drove down the two-lane state route. My hair was a bit jacked, but I played with it enough to get it back in place and presentable for the ladies.

That was when my eyes returned to the highway and I noticed we were halfway across the opposite lane. I freaked. I jerked the wheel strongly back to our side and as the car began to switch back into our lane, it rocked as if we were in a bouncy house. That was when I realized I had over corrected and I quickly turned the wheel back to the left. The car again bounced back to the other side and I began to fear that I was going to roll it, flying down the highway at fifty-five miles per hour. I quickly jerked it back to the right, trying not to over correct, but at this point I was about to lose full control. That was when I remembered that I was driving my parent's car. It was a smaller car and front wheel drive.

This was the car I used to slide around corners and pulled the emergency brake. Whenever I slid around corners and I wanted to quickly recover, I let go of the wheel and pressed on the gas. The car would begin to autocorrect and the front wheels would pull the rest of the car forward and it would straighten out. *This was my only chance,* I thought, *before I roll the vehicle, flying down the highway.* I quickly let go of the steering wheel and kept my foot on the gas. Then Steve freaked out.

"What are you doing?! Grab the wheel!!" he screamed. It didn't take long before the car stopped swaying and the front wheels began to autocorrect the car into a forward motion, reducing the sway to the left and right. We were still somewhat on the opposite side of the highway, but no cars were coming at us from the other direction. The car finally shimmered out completely and I regained control of the wheel and the car at the same time. At that point, I let off the gas and slowly steered back into our lane. I pulled the car slowly over to the side of the road and we sat there for a moment staring off into outer space. We were both stunned and not sure how we survived.

"I think we better go home," I suggested.

"Sounds good," Steve replied. "I think I need to go change my pants anyway." We both burst out laughing, turned the car around and went home. Steve and I had so many adventures that I could write another book about just those. We developed a close bond and a friendship that I had never experienced in my life. We had many of the same goals and desires in life. We also had similar ways to handle them. We became more and more like each other, the way that teenage friends have a tendency to do. I am sure I became more like him than he ever did me, but it didn't matter because I loved so much about him.

The following Fall, Steve and I both played football for our eight-man tackle football team. I didn't grow much, I remained small at about a hundred and twenty-five pounds. Steve became our starting tailback and I became the fourth-string fullback. If you are not familiar with football, the tailback is the star running back that everyone knows. Famous tailbacks had names you are probably familiar with, like O.J. Simpson, Barry Sanders and Walter Payton. The unknown fullbacks in the NFL that blocked for those tailbacks were Larry Watkins, Tommy Vardell, and Matt Suhey respectively. Fullback was not only an underappreciated position, but I was fourth-string on a team that didn't have three backups at any other position. Nevertheless, I used it to get in shape for wrestling and had a lot of fun playing on the JV team.

In our lone state playoff game that year at the end of the season, I found myself doing what I did best for our team. I followed the plays on the sideline and screamed words of encouragement. I was our biggest cheerleader, hoping that would put me in good graces with our coach, enough for him to pity me and put me in once in a while. However, this usually only happened if we were up thirty or more points, which actually happened more often that season than you might imagine.

On this particular afternoon, I was doing just that. I was running up and down the sideline, yelling when I didn't notice a hole in the ground. My foot went into that hole. My body went completely off-kilter and I rolled my ankle. I hit the ground quickly and to my relief, everyone else had been watching the play and didn't see me make a fool of myself as I fell to the ground.

I was injured in action as our team cheerleading captain. I was so embarrassed. Of course, this shifted my attention from how our team was struggling, to trying to walk off my painful ankle injury. We went into half-time, down fifteen points and one tortured ankle on my part.

We continued to struggle as a team in the second half. Our starting fullback was athletically gifted and would periodically get the ball to run, instead of being used as a traditional fullback, blocking or in short yardage situations. He fumbled the ball twice and continued to try and run it to the outside instead of settling for short yardage up the middle. Coach got so upset, he put in our backup who was just a freshman, but also physically gifted and as tough as they came. It wasn't long before he got hurt and Coach opted for our third stringer, a sophomore who was also physically gifted, but didn't practice the position often. He was a starter on defense and began to struggle in the fullback role, fumbling once himself.

In a strange turn of events, we intercepted a pass and returned it for a touchdown. No one else was ready on offense, except for me, "the cheerleading captain." Though I was small and slow, coach knew I would follow my blocks so he had me go in to try for the two-point conversion after the touchdown. He even called my number on a play called "24-hit." That meant I got the ball and followed my blocks up the middle to the right. I did just that and actually scored the conversion! Coach liked what he saw and when we got the ball back starting the fourth quarter and down eight points, he called my number.

"Congleton, get in there!" Coach yelled. I couldn't believe it. He was letting me play. In a playoff game we were losing, but was still within reach. I did exactly what he said as quickly as I could. And he continued to call my number by calling plays where I would run the ball up the middle either on the left or the right side. Our linemen in front of me were all pretty big and very solid. I followed my blocks the best I could and it went well! I was picking up three, four or five yards each carry.

No more, no less. I ran left. I ran right. Before I knew it, we had made it up the entire field and I carried it into the endzone for a touchdown with just seconds to go in the game. The game was tied, but we didn't have a kicker for an easy extra point to win. We had to go for two and Coach put me back in the game. He called a timeout to discuss the details.

When we reached the huddle, Coach said, "Alright we are going to run '24-hit' again, except this time Congleton is going to get the ball directly up the middle. Palmer is going to take the hike, step to his left and hand the ball to Congleton who is going to run right up the center behind Luke. You got it?! Let's go!" I couldn't believe it. Not only was I getting to play in a meaningful game, but I had been a major part of our comeback AND Coach was calling a special play just for me. I had to come through!

We went back on the field and set up for the play. Palmer, our quarterback, announced the start of the play by saying "hut, hut." I dropped my right hand into the dirt and looked up at the line in front of me. "Hike!" Everyone moved in a blur of motion as I saw Palmer take the hike and move his body to our left. He reached the ball out to my right and I sprinted my slow sprint to the ball where I creased my forearms around the ball and pulled it into my belly trying to hide the fact that I was keeping it. The defense *knew* I was getting the ball and came after me. I did my best to run right behind Luke and sprinted toward the goal line where I knew the winning score was waiting. Right as I reached Luke's back end, I felt the defense smack into my shoulder pads. I also saw the line which was only a foot in front of me.

I held the ball deep in my stomach and began churning my legs driving toward the end zone line. I was close, very close. I knew I was almost there, but I had to be sure. I reached the ball out toward the goal line before they brought me down. As I reached it out, I realized that I wasn't making any forward progress any more as my body was starting to move in the opposite direction. I squirmed and turned, literally rotating my body with my belly toward the sky and I lifted the ball in front of me toward the goal line. As I reached the ball out, I felt my body hit the ground landing on my back with the ball stretched out in front of me. Once I laid fully on the ground, I turned to look for the line. The ball laid just beyond the line! *I did it! We won the game!* I thought.

That was when the whistle blew and the ref yelled, "He's down! No score!" I looked over and saw the ref pointing to the ground and my knee, saying that it was down before the ball crossed the line. I couldn't believe it! I knew I had scored! They ripped the win right out of my chest! But I was ready for overtime.

We flipped a coin for each team to have one opportunity in overtime. We got the ball second. We stopped them in four tries. Now it was our turn and we got the ball at the twenty-five yard line. That was when all hope left my body. Coach yelled for our starting fullback to get back in the game. He called several similar plays as earlier in the game with the same similar results. Our starter tried running outside and went nowhere. We were stopped on four plays in familiar fashion. The other team scored on their next possession and the game was over. We lost. To this day, I swear, I scored. The ref saw it another way and my story ended differently than I wrote it up in my mind.

Steve was my biggest cheerleader. If ever I questioned my athletic abilities at something, he reminded me of that playoff game and how I crushed it in the fourth quarter. We enjoyed many experiences together in those two years and we made decisions that would alter our lives forever. He joined me working at the Golden Spike Inn, washing dishes, where we got fired together for having a match fight in the dining room. We skipped school together often and bad-mouthed teachers sometimes while we were in the same class. I lived in his garage after graduation. We fought over girls, but never let it split up our friendship. The biggest decision that changed our lives though was when he decided to join the Marine Corps with me on the buddy program.

Chapter 21

Senior Year and Beyond (1990-1992)

My senior year of wrestling started out with a bang because my dad wanted to move again. I ran away. I threatened to live with Steve until I graduated. I think Dad didn't want to lose me the way he lost Jimmy and Terri so he decided to stay. We didn't move and I came home from Steve's.

I had a great beginning to my senior year of wrestling and I won my first tournament in Bennett. This was the first tournament that my Bart Simpson doll sat matside with me. The coach's daughter had sewed up a wrestling singlet and headgear for my doll. When I went out to wrestle, I sat him right next to the coach's chair in the corner of the mat. I imagined him cheering me on and giving me power. I beat my first opponent easily, pinning him in the first period.

My second opponent wrestled for Bennett and I heard he was a pretty good wrestler. A couple of kids from the next town over offered me twenty bucks to hurt him. I smiled, but declined and said that I had planned to just beat him badly instead. When we got out on the mat to wrestle, I quickly learned why he was so good. He was very strong and stout. He had a solid base, but I was able to take him down in the first period and held a two to one lead moving into the second period after he escaped my control. He chose "down" at the beginning of the second period and I knew I had to break his base flat and not let him escape or the score would be tied up.

As soon as the whistle blew, I took my right arm and popped his right arm off the mat while taking my left hand and forced his left leg off it's base. This caused him to lose two of his four points of base and his body flopped to the mat with his ribs smacking hard and sudden. He let out a loud grunt of agony, but I knew I had to drive him if I was going to have a chance to turn him on his back to pin him so I kept moving hard and fast. The ref blew his whistle and finally I pulled back. As I removed myself off of him, he remained on the mat grunting in pain. After a few minutes, a trainer came out to the mat and escorted him off. The referee declared me the winner since he could not finish the match and my move that led to his injury was completely legal.

That win put me in the finals and I was pumped! I thought later that I should have tried to collect that money for hurting him, but it was an obvious coincidence as I never meant to actually hurt him. My finals match went quicker than I thought since I was able to pin my opponent at the beginning of the third period to win my first tournament! I was stoked because he had been a state qualifier the year before and had beaten me in a previous tournament. I still remember, after the tournament they escorted us to these boxes where we stood, indicating our tournament place. I was wearing my typical Bart

Simpson t-shirt for my warm up. I stepped up to the top step and raised my Bart doll over my head while holding my winning tournament brackets lower in my other hand as if to indicate where my strength came from.

The following week, I won my second tournament. This time in my *hometown* of Byers, if that's what you could call it. The season continued in spectacular fashion, but I hoped to get my revenge against Ty Freel in a tournament hosted by our neighboring town, Strasburg. Unfortunately, Ty moved up to the one hundred twenty-five pound weight class and wouldn't drop back to my weight to wrestle me. I considered moving up, but never did. We never wrestled again, though I always wondered if I had improved enough to beat him. I made it to state again my senior year and finished with a record of twenty-four wins and only six losses.

Dad never did come to another wrestling match after the one at state my junior year, though Mom stopped at another one on her way home my senior year. At state, I was lucky enough to get matched up against Jonah Olguin again for my second match. I won my first match giving me the opportunity to face Jonah, but he pinned me in the second period again. That time, he pinned me in the head and arm that I had avoided the previous year. I won my next match in the consolation round, winning in three periods by a score of seven to three. I had to win one more match and I was guaranteed to place somewhere between third through sixth. At this point in the tournament, if I won the next match, I was going to be pitted against a wrestler who had placed at state the year prior and had beaten me twice that season in two very close matches.

Unfortunately, I came out focused on my next match because before I knew what had happened, I had been taken down and almost pinned. I was quickly down five to zero. I wrestled valiantly the rest of the match, but I was stunned. I lost seven to three to finish my wrestling career. After shaking my opponent's and his coach's hand, I returned to my corner and fell down on my face and just lost it. I started bawling right there in the middle of McNichol's Arena with ten mats on the floor full of wrestlers and fifteen thousand people in the stands. My wrestling career was over and I lost right before placing at the state tournament. I knew I should have placed and I was distraught. My coach lifted me up and told me to pull myself together and get off the mat.

In a surprising twist, my dad offered me an olive branch unlike any other. He offered to take me back to Rip Griffin's Truck Stop to eat All-You-Can-Eat Steak as a consolation prize for not placing at state. I had been cutting six or seven pounds every week for months to remain in my weight class. I was ready to eat. Many teenagers might have gone out and gotten drunk to wallow in their pity, but I went out and ate to my heart's content. Dad and I had a competition that night and he thought it would be easy to beat me because I had a shrunken stomach from not eating much. Dad ate *eight*, eight-ounce steaks! We didn't eat anything else. No fries, no rolls, no salad, nothing. We only ate the meat. I beat him though, after eating *nine* eight ounce steaks! I found out later that he had wrapped one of his in a napkin and snuck it into my mom's purse to try and beat me. We were always so competitive and it seemed I was the only one in the family who could ever beat him at anything. That night though, unlike the night of pool when he was drunk, he just laughed it off and was happy for me.

That spring of my senior year, I decided to play baseball instead of running track. Our town had a community baseball team for years, but that was the first year our high school played baseball. I thought I had a chance to play and it seemed like fun. A couple of weeks into the season, I found my place as the back-up second baseman to one of our talented sophomores. After a few weeks, Coach told me to go out into the outfield during practice. After practice, I left my uniform at his office door and never returned. That was the only time I ever quit. I accepted not being able to start or get much playing time since I didn't have a lot of experience, but I figured if I wasn't even able to even *practice* at my position, what was the point?! Instead, I decided to try club freestyle wrestling to prepare for college where I wanted to try and walk on the wrestling team.

Time flew by that spring and before I knew it, graduation came! I was elated that I finally graduated. In many ways, it meant so much to me and I'm sure my parents too, even though they never vocalized it. I was the first kid in our family to graduate while still living at home. I had definitely accomplished something. I had also forced my parents to not move again, something that hadn't happened before that, no matter how many times Jimmy ran away. I graduated at seventeen years old and didn't turn eighteen until the third week of July.

Regardless, I moved out immediately and lived in Steve's garage that summer. I was finally free of my dad's terror! He no longer had any say in my life. I hated that man so much and couldn't stand to be around him any longer than I had to be, for certain family situations after that.

That fall, I drove myself up to the University of Northern Colorado in Greeley to start college. My parents never helped me apply, never helped me with the Free Application for Student Aid (FAFSA), and never helped me transition to college in any way. I was planning to be a computer programmer and on my drive up to college I began to dream about how I was going to use that education. *How cool would that be,* I thought, *if you could input into the computer what town you were leaving and what town you were traveling to and it would tell you the best route to get there?!* The following year, Rand McNally released their first CD-ROM maps that allowed people to do just that. I missed my opportunity at being a millionaire!

College was a great experience! The best part was that I was on my own, away from my dad. No longer did I have to deal with him belittling me and live under the threat of physical violence. I quickly made friends at college and we did a lot of typical college things. We partied every weekend, though I still didn't drink or do drugs. I just hung out with everyone else while they did. We did crazy things in our dorm like stacking all of the couch cushions and jumping on them like they were a trampoline. I had two computer programming classes back to back at 8 and 9 a.m. I slept in way too often or showed up for the 8 a.m. class and then went out on the lawn and slept through the 9 a.m. class. Needless to say, my college experience was fun, but I wasn't very successful academically. I was way too immature and irresponsible.

Thanksgiving rolled around and I planned to go home for the holiday since everyone else did too. About that same time, I received a report that showed I was failing four of my five classes. I also received notice from the bursar that I owed the college over fifteen hundred dollars. Apparently, I failed to sign some loan papers and my student loans didn't go through. I didn't have the cash, obviously, so I decided to drop out of college at Thanksgiving. I moved in with my sister Terri who still lived in Deer Trail, just twelve miles from Byers. I also got a job with her at Arby's in Limon. We drove over thirty miles to work at Arby's, but it was a job and an easy one at that. After working as a short order cook, fast-food was easy for me.

One Saturday evening, Dad came over to Terri's house when I was living with them. He was upset with her husband, Gary, about something. I tried to defend Gary, even though he probably deserved it. I always hated to see my dad treat people like crap. Dad was drunk and running his mouth about something when he got in my face and started to get physical. I had nowhere to go and was pressed up against the table. My wrestling instincts kicked in and I took him down to his back and clasped his arms together. I couldn't believe he was trying to put his hands on me as an adult. I couldn't stand this man, but I didn't hit him. I just held him in place. Mom was there and again, told me to let him go. Finally, I let him up and walked out. I had enough of him and had no plans to ever see him again.

I lived with my sister Terri and her husband Gary for six or seven months working at Arby's. I had an easy job and was proficient at it, but I knew that wasn't my long term future. I also knew I was still too immature and irresponsible to go back to college right away, not to mention I couldn't afford it. I needed to grow up and I needed to become more responsible. I needed money for college if I ever was going to go back, so I decided to do what made the most sense to me.

I joined the Marine Corps because I knew that would force me to grow up and become responsible real quick. I also knew that I could take advantage of the G.I. Bill and it would help me pay for college once I was ready.

Shortly after I signed up, Steve graduated high school. He was a year behind me and we were hanging out at his house one day talking about our summer plans with our other friend, Brian.

"I'm going back to Ohio for the summer," Steve explained.

"Why? Man, it's going to be so boring here without you!" I exclaimed.

"Yeah, what's up man? I thought we were brutherrrrs," Brian said.

"Heidi and I started dating long distance and I want to see her! Man, she is so fine!" Steve said.

"Come on man, girls can't break up the brotherhood!" I pleaded.

"Wait," Steve said, "why don't you guys come with me?!"

"What? How can we do that? Where would we stay?" Brian asked.

"Who cares? We'll figure it out. My dad will let you stay. And if he doesn't we could probably stay at Heidi's brother's house. He lives just a few houses down from her!" Steve explained.

"What do you think?" I asked Brian.

"I don't know. Seems kinda lame. There any brown girls out there?" Brian asked. Brian had moved into a suburb of Denver that was known to have a high hispanic population and only dated mexican girls now.

"I don't know about that, but there are plenty of fine girls in Springfield!" Steve said.

"Now that sounds like the best thing I've heard yet," I responded. "Let's do it!"

"How are we gonna get there?" Brian asked. "I don't trust Cong's hoopty."

"Yeah, not sure my car would make it," I responded.

"Your car, man!" Steve explained to Brian. "Come on, Shawn and I will pay for the gas!" That took me back. *Wait, I have to pay for the gas?!* I wondered.

"I don't know if I have the money for that," I said.

"Come on you guys, this is the brotherhood, we got to do this!" Steve begged. Finally, Brian caved and we did it. We drove on Interstate 70 from Byers, Colorado to Springfield, Ohio almost twelve hundred miles.

About halfway there, the three of us got into an argument. Brian was so mad, he tried to pull off the road and wanted to turn the car around. Sitting on the side of the highway, Steve talked me into just telling him what he wanted to hear so that we could at least get there. We agreed we would figure out how to get home later. He was sure his dad would give us a bus ride home if nothing else. I calmed down and together Steve and I calmed Brian down. We were able to talk him into finishing the trip. Shortly after arriving in Springfield, Brian got upset again and drove back to Byers on his own. We were left in Ohio without a vehicle, but Steve had connections and we found our way around. That summer in Springfield was the beginning of my life changing for good.

Chapter 22

Springfield, Ohio (Summer 1992)

Steve's dad was the youth pastor of their church, High Street Church of the Nazarene in Springfield. While I had very little experience in church prior to this, we found ourselves attending church or youth group at least three times a week. Oddly enough, this didn't bother me. Maybe it was because there were plenty of girls at youth group that I quickly became interested in. Maybe it was because Steve was almost a bit of a celebrity there with his dad being the youth pastor. Maybe it was because Steve's girlfriend at least *tried* to hook me up with one of her friends so I didn't annoy them as a third wheel. Whatever it was, I enjoyed it. Steve's dad was a lot of fun too and a bit charismatic, much like Steve. I saw where he got it.

I specifically remember that I enjoyed singing songs at church even though they didn't mean much to me personally. We sang, "Our God is an Awesome God," and no one got into it more than me. I imagine much of it had to do with the fact that I loved music. Dad always instilled a love for music into us. And I loved to sing along when the melody was catchy. Most of the church songs were very catchy and they put the words up on a screen to help us sing along, kind of like karaoke. That helped me a lot because I never really knew many of the words to songs when I tried to sing along with a radio station.

We stayed with Steve's dad some and with Heidi's older brother some. Since we didn't have wheels, Heidi's brother's house was much more convenient because it was only a few houses down from Heidi's house. He had MTV, so that was great when we were bored! But we spent a lot of time at Heidi's house and I was left being a third wheel far too often. Thankfully, two other people saved me from my boredom. Heidi had a sister named Holly that was four years younger than her so I hung out with her a lot. She was much younger and not my type so I wasn't interested romantically, but she was at least someone to hang out with. Also, Heidi's mom, Rosemary was around most of the time and she welcomed me into the family.

I thought of Rosemary as an older lady, close to my parents age, but she was so full of life! She was always interested in having fun and was warm, kind and welcoming. She made me feel like a million bucks, like I was the most important person on earth. She had a gift for loving teenagers and I was a teenager who needed love. She quickly became like a second mom to me, even more than Cathy ever was. While Cathy was nice and welcoming into the family, she always seemed a bit impersonal, like she had to because I was Steve's friend. Rosemary's way of bringing me into the family was to treat me like I was her son. She was affectionate with hugs, compliments and lots of laughs.

Steve and Heidi spent a lot of time "intertwining" as Rosemary put it, laying around with their legs wrapped or their arms overlapped or holding hands with their bodies closely aligned. Heidi's family was very religious so nothing beyond that was ever allowed and I could tell her mom wasn't too happy with that either. Though Rosemary was religious, she listened to the stories of my life and was simply amazed that I ever survived. She treated me like I was a lost war hero and was worthy of honor and a meritorious award. It felt great to have someone know about my life and appreciate me and what I went through. Steve was probably the only other person at that time in my life who had done that. Rosemary and I often hung out near the kitchen talking while Steve and Heidi intertwined in the living room. While I shared stories about my life, she shared stories about Jesus, the church and her own life.

While I didn't have much experience with church growing up, churches had helped out a bit with our moves across the country. I also spent a short time attending church in the second grade when my parents were divorced and then a short stint in 7th grade with a youth group in the mountains when we lived in Bailey, Colorado. I didn't exactly have a real positive view of church despite these experiences. It seemed rather constricting to me with all of their rules.

In fact, I had quite the foul mouth during my teenage years and I found myself cussing up a storm when we were in church or hanging out with the youth group. Steve would warn me at times about talking like that in church, but I didn't really care. I said things the way I wanted to say them, at least around the other teenagers. Besides, whenever I cussed, people seemed to notice me more and listened as if I was saying something more important. Cussing caught their attention and made me feel more important.

I did watch my mouth around the adults though and tried to keep it clean around Rosemary or Steve's dad. I don't remember if I ever slipped around them, but if I did, they were gracious about it and didn't come down on me. Outside of my conversations with Rosemary, we spent most of our time with Heidi, one of her friends, and/or other youth group members. Attending church and/or youth group three times a week opened me up to a message that I was really hearing for the first time in my life. I may have heard it prior to that, but this was the first time that I was *really hearing* it.

"God sent his only son that whosoever believes in Him should not perish, but have everlasting life." That message hit me in a way that struck me odd. *God would sacrifice his son? For me? What did I do to deserve this?* I wondered. *If God loved his own son, why would he sacrifice him? Why would he kill his own son? Was this really the only way?* I was left with so many questions. Sometimes things I heard at church made sense, other times not so much. I loved the idea of grace. People would love me even though they didn't know me and I did nothing to deserve it. *Who wouldn't love that?!* I thought.

One reason I was able to fit right into the youth group was the fact that they were a pretty informal church. As teenagers, we could get away with wearing jeans or shorts to church and no one cared. They didn't look down on us nor say anything to us about it. I thought that was pretty cool for a church. My dad always instilled a real sense of informal dress and I hated to dress up any more than wearing jeans. We didn't have to and that helped me feel more accepted at church.

However, the biggest reason I probably felt most accepted was simply because I was. By everyone. The older people at the church were very friendly and open to me being at church even though I was pretty clueless about what was going on there. The youth group kids immediately became my friends. They included me in everything and there were a couple of girls in the youth group that I was interested in. More importantly, they seemed just as interested in me. Both Steve's dad (the youth pastor) and the senior pastor of the church accepted me, joked around with me and treated me as if I had been there forever. *If they only knew what my life had been like,* I thought.

My dad made my life a living hell, I thought. *How could a **loving** God allow that to happen? How could this God love me? Did he even know what my thought life was like? Had he heard the way I talked? No way this God could love me. That's great for all these churchy people who had lived **Disney** lives, but my life was like from a different world.* I felt like we were from different planets. Sure, churches helped our family at times. Terri even went when she was in a foster home and she told me she liked it, but Jimmy did too and he hated it.

I was definitely challenged with this new message in my life that God loved me and he sent his son to die for me. I learned that if I would repent of my sins and put my faith in Jesus, I could inherit eternal life. *Seriously?* I wondered. *Everything I had done wrong in my life would be forgiven? That's all it took was to say I was sorry? Then I could go to heaven?* It seemed too good to be true and not very realistic, at least not for me. I didn't live in that fairy tale land.

I lived in a very real world, where dads beat their kids and worse (to me), these dads told them how terrible they were. "You're not good enough and you never will be," were words etched in my mind. In my world, dads cussed out their kids and took everything they ever cared about away from them. In my world, you didn't stick around anywhere long enough to build real friendships that lasted. In my world, even family left when it got hard. *I don't know where these people are from,* I thought, *but they aren't from my world and they have no idea what it's been like to live in my world.*

Later that summer, Steve started asking me questions about the Marine Corps. I had already gone to MEPS (Military Entrance Processing Station) in Denver and had been approved to go. I had even already signed my contract. I was set to leave for bootcamp from Denver, Colorado on Monday, September 14, 1992. Steve told me that he was planning to propose to Heidi who was still only going into her junior year of high school. He didn't think he would have enough money to get married and live together after high school if he went to college so he was thinking of joining the Marine Corps so they could get married after she graduated and they could start a life together. We talked about possibly joining together on the buddy program so we went down to the recruiter's office in Springfield.

Steve's mom was in the Air Force so I was a bit surprised he was thinking about joining the Marine Corps with me. He definitely seemed more like the *chAir Force* type. He was softer and while he was able to make it through football okay, didn't really seem like he would have made it through a wrestling season. *He was also a bit preppy to be a Marine,* I thought.

I had put up with my dad who was a jerk my whole life, I could easily deal with the Marine Corps, I thought. The reputation of the Marine Corps was appealing to me since I considered them the hardest and the baddest of the military services. My dad had been a Marine and Jimmy, my older brother had become a Marine. *I could become a Marine too!* I thought. No taking the easy way out for me.

Steve, however, had the same thought. *If Shawn can do it, I can definitely do it,* he thought. We found out that Steve could indeed join me on the buddy program, but he had to do it from Colorado. He couldn't commit while still in Ohio. He had to join from Denver, like I did. If he had committed from Springfield, he would have had to go to bootcamp at Parris Island in South Carolina since he would be joining east of the Mississippi River. But I was already slated for bootcamp in San Diego. While I was interested in going to Parris Island since Dad told me that was where he went, I wasn't interested in changing my start date to a later date to accommodate that. I was ready to move on with the rest of my life. I found freedom from my family, particularly my dad, but now I needed the freedom to support myself financially.

That summer, I ended up dating a couple of Heidi's friends from the youth group. One girl I dated for more than a month, but we ended up breaking up near the end of the summer and I started to date one of her other friends just weeks before we went back to Colorado. Springfield, Ohio had been good to me. I found a lot of friends in the youth group.

While I hadn't exactly accepted this hard to believe message the church preached to me, I did enjoy the acceptance I found from people there. They sure seemed like a second, much better family than I had growing up! I really enjoyed that summer in Springfield and it set me on a path toward a changed life. I had been introduced to this guy, Jesus, and he was intriguing. He was quite possibly, too good to be true.

Near the end of the summer, Steve proposed to Heidi and she accepted. He decided to join me on the buddy program and go to bootcamp with me as soon as we got home to Colorado. Though I had just started dating another of Heidi's friends, I told her that I would write to her everyday and we could date from afar. She was up for it and we did.

At the end of the summer, we gave our goodbye hugs and they sent us off back to Colorado. I called home to my parents before we went and they told me that they were moving from Colorado to Texas. They wanted our help to move them so they sent money for a Greyhound bus ticket for us to come back to Colorado.

We rode the Greyhound back, which took us more than twenty-four hours. When we got back, we loaded all of my family's belongings into a moving truck. This was the first time in our entire lives that I remember actually using a moving truck. By this time, my dad's record collection had grown to over seventeen thousand albums and eight thousand forty-fives. He had started to collect CDs, as well. Mom had grown her own book collection and our VCR tape collection had also grown to almost a thousand tapes. The only way they were going to be able to keep their collection was to rent a truck. Mom requested a transfer at her insurance company to Austin, Texas and they approved it.

When Steve and I got back to Colorado, the first place we went was to the recruiter's office to get Steve signed up. Things progressed quickly and he was able to get the same enlistment date and we were promised we would be in the same platoon in boot camp. We returned to a house in the country near Byers where my parents had moved after I graduated high school. We loaded them up and I helped move them by driving the rental truck to Texas while Mom and Dad both drove one of their two cars. Dad got another DUI shortly before leaving and was afraid to drive again. But he joked that they couldn't take his license anyway since he didn't have one to begin with.

Shortly after arriving in Texas, I helped them unload and they bussed me back to Colorado. I sometimes wonder why I helped them move, yet again. I was free and didn't have to, but I probably promised to help just so they would bus us back from Ohio. Nevertheless, I did help them move to Texas, though I quickly returned to Colorado to be free of them again and to start my future.

Steve and I got a ride into Denver by his mom on Sunday, September 13, 1992. We were put up in a hotel room that night near the airport. The following morning we flew out of Denver to San Diego to begin our military career which would change the trajectory of both of our lives.

Chapter 23

MCRD San Diego (1992)

"Get off the bus! Get off the bus!" the drill instructor screamed.

"Aye, aye, sir!" we all responded in unison. About fifty young men from all different walks of life joined me by emptying that white non-descript bus onto the yellow footprints located on the pavement.

"10, 9, 8, 7, 6, 5, 4, 3, 2, 1," screamed another drill instructor waiting for us outside of the bus. "You are now aboard Marine Corps Recruit Depot, San Diego!"

"Yes, sir!" we all responded together. By now, we filled the yellow footprints that were formed on the ground in a formation that we were unfamiliar with, but not for long.

"You have just taken the first step in becoming a member of the world's finest fighting force, the United States Marine

Corps!" he yelled. "You should be standing at the position of attention."

We all stiffened up our bodies as much as possible. Our arms lay at our side with our hands clenched and our thumbs centered on the side of our trousers. Our feet were close together at our heels, but our toes faced about forty five degrees away from each other. Our eyes and head were faced forward, being careful not to make eye contact with the drill instructor in front of us. It was dark, but we could see through the light and we knew he could see us. We prayed that he wouldn't, but we readied ourselves for whatever was next.

"Get your butts inside!" yelled another drill instructor as he approached our group from behind. Those in the front row of our group quickly began to move by briskly walking forward into the building. The double doors were open and waiting for us to enter. Inside we saw another set of yellow footprints on the floor and quickly moved to cover those up with our feet.

"Listen up, you maggots. You are going to be issued your gear, compliments of the United States Marine Corps. You will secure your gear and you will take care of it. Do you understand?!" screamed another drill instructor that had been waiting for us inside.

"Yes, sir!" we all yelled again. It was five in the morning and the sun had yet to rise, but we were all waking up quickly. We were alert and ready for anything or so we thought. The next forty eight hours consisted of hurrying up – or scurrying up to be more accurate – waiting in line and receiving our gear. This was processing and we didn't sleep for forty eight hours. We looked like a bunch of numbskulls running from place to place and really had no idea how to line up, how to march or how to wear our newly issued gear. We were clueless and this left us on the wrong end of screaming terror erupting from the drill instructors' mouths.

Initially, Steve and I were side by side as often as possible. Our last names were close since he was a Coffman and I was a Congleton so that helped out initially. However, we were quickly assigned our place in the platoon based on height. Steve was much taller and the taller guys lined up in the front of the platoon. As one of the shorter guys, I was almost always in the back of the formation. Being in the back of the platoon had its advantages and disadvantages.

When we entered the chow hall, that meant I was one of the last to go in. The drill instructors had a saying, "When the first recruit is done, you're all done." This meant I usually got about two minutes to eat. For the most part that didn't bother me too much because I was a quick eater in my family, but the two minutes weren't long and I quickly became an even faster eater. There was no talking allowed and our eyes and heads were down, focused on eating our food.

The advantage, however, was that I was often hidden in the back. I made it my number one goal to blend in and not stand out. If I was successful, I didn't draw the attention and therefore, the wrath of a drill instructor who was trying to shape me into being a man or more poignantly, a Marine. Thankfully, I was pretty successful and throughout boot camp, there were only two times that a drill instructor addressed me individually. The group badgering was bad enough though.

We signed a contract and technically became Marines the day we stepped onto that recruit depot, we thought. However, our drill instructors were very clear that we hadn't earned that title yet, we were simply *recruits* to them. They spent the next thirteen weeks tearing us down and reteaching us how to live life. Every moment of every day was structured into some form of indoctrination into the life of a Marine. We were only in processing for a couple of days and then we were handed off to our drill instructors that would be with us throughout the entirety of our training. This was a surprise to us at the time since we didn't realize those first drill instructors we encountered would be passing us off. That was both a relief and a wake up call in itself. We were glad to be free of a few that we feared the most, but were also given one that we truly feared, one that we truly respected and one that we kinda laughed at (mostly in our heads only – *mostly*). Except for that one time.

Boot camp was broken into three phases, each lasted four weeks. A couple of weeks into our first phase, we had just been issued our rifles and were going through safety checks and learning how to hold the weapon while in formation. While I was checking out my weapon, I had not been listening to the instructions of the drill instructor when he arrived near me.

As he started to pass by, Sergeant Abolins screamed, "What the h*ll are you doing, Conjeltun?!" I stopped looking at my weapon and just held it in the air where I froze my body as if I could become invisible. "Well, what the h*ll are you doing?!" he asked again since I didn't answer him.

"Sir, this recruit didn't hear your instructions," I yelled with his face near inches from mine. I don't know why we all kept yelling, but it was par for the course. Our communication was loud and affirmative. This kind of reminded me of home. Dad was the loudest person we knew and we all followed suit. Of course, we never tried to outdo him in that regard, but the louder he got, the louder we got. Sergeant Abolins' mouth scrunched up and his face squeezed together like he had just eaten the most sour lemon ever. He was the one we laughed at, in our heads, until that moment.

"You are dead! Do you understand that?! You are dead! If you don't hear my instructions in battle, you are dead! What is wrong with you Conjeltoe?!" At that moment, I couldn't help it, I burst out laughing. I was filled with fear, but my *humorous* bone was struck hard. He gave it his best effort to be hard and mean. He was just silly. We could all see right through him. He was a bit of a joke. That was also a new version of my name that I had never heard before.

"Get your *ss over to the sand pit!" he yelled. We were in the barracks, but the front portion of our barracks held a space where they would *slay* us individually or in smaller groups. Slaying was reminiscent of wrestling drills. It wasn't so much the physical portion of the workout that bothered me, but the drill instructors got in my face the entire time and screamed some form of obscenities at me. This moment was also exceptional because he used the word *ss. Drill instructors technically weren't allowed to cuss so they would use words like butt, friggin and dang instead of the actual cuss words. Sergeant Abolins was trying to prove how hard he was by breaking protocol to use an actual cuss word.

I quickly ran to the front of the barracks and started running in place with my knees high and my rifle held at chest height. "Get down and push!" he yelled as he followed me to the front. I set my weapon on the ground and started to do push-ups. He leaned down toward my head and continued to yell, "you good for nothing, piece of crap! You expect to be a Marine?! You can't even listen to simple instructions. What is wrong with you?!" I pushed and pushed, but now I was starting to lose it emotionally. The laughter that let loose inside a few moments ago started to feign and I was quickly reminded of my dad. He yelled many of those same things at me only with much more profanity.

"Get up! Run! High knees!" he continued. I stood up and started to run with high knees as he continued. "Where is your weapon?! How can you leave your weapon on the ground?! I don't want you in my platoon! You are going to get us all killed! Pick your weapon up!" I reached back down and grabbed my weapon off the floor and held it chest high and started to lift my knees again. From that point on, my mind connected the brutish drill instructors with my dad. *Physically*, I was more than capable of handling the experience. *Emotionally*, I became distraught.

Throughout the first phase of boot camp, the drill instructors constantly asked guys while yelling at them and slaying them if they wanted out. They would antagonize them or pretend to sympathize with them as if we had a choice in the matter. We all signed up with a contract and the only way out was a discharge that was less than honorable. None of us knew how that might affect us the rest of our lives so we weighed the fear of a dishonorable discharge with the fear of our drill instructor yelling at us. Some recruits took the bait and said they wanted out in moments of weakness. This typically resulted in further humiliation and badgering by the drill instructors.

Once in a while, shortly after that experience a guy would come up missing and leave the platoon. None of us knew what that meant. *Did they go AWOL (Absent With Out Leave)? Were they discharged? Did they drop into a new platoon that was a week or two behind?* we wondered. The fear of not knowing kept most of us in line and we pressed on in our training.

The second phase of our preparation required us to transport about forty five miles north from San Diego to Camp Pendleton for field training. We were issued new gear which included tents, sleeping bags and combat gear like kevlar helmets and flak jackets. At Camp Pendleton, we spent a couple of weeks learning how to shoot our rifles and qualifying with them. After rifle qualification, we set out on the longest hump of our training which was about eighteen miles. A *hump* is a hike that includes about seventy five to a hundred pounds of gear including our weapons, kevlar helmets, and full packs.

We began our hike at the barracks and moved into the wilderness. Unfortunately for me, we lined up in height order again, just like our regular platoon formation. This meant I was in the rear of the formation when we began. This was even more challenging because of the format of our hump. As we hiked, each recruit was required to closely follow the recruit in front of them. If a larger space formed between them because a recruit could not keep up, they were directed to drop out of the formation and fall back to the rear of the platoon. That meant that the next recruit had to quickly fill the gap, causing every recruit behind to pick up the pace to fill the gap.

Since I started pretty far in the back, I was required to pick up the pace and fill the gap every time a recruit fell back. We maintained a challenging pace to begin with. This only exasperated the pace even more for me. About two-thirds of the way through the eighteen mile hike at about mile thirteen, we reached the Reaper. The Reaper was a peak on the highest hill at Camp Pendleton. At the point we reached the top, all but four guys had fallen back and I was almost at the very front near Steve. However, we took a short break at that point and lined back up in our original spots.

From that point on, we went downhill until we reached the beach. Normally, I loved to go to the beach. The ocean smell was amazing and the seagull sounds were refreshing and peaceful. However, this was quite a different experience since we had about a mile to hike on the beach in thick sand. For every step forward, it felt like we were falling back a half-step. We were also more than three fourths of the way through the hike at about mile fifteen. Once we exited the beach, we headed back to the barracks. Our feet were mush and our legs were more than wobbly. We were exhausted, but we made it! The most physical portion of our training was over!

A few days later, we were continuing our physical training. I can't imagine that I would have been able to complete this training without my sports background. Wrestling and football definitely prepared me for the physical nature of this training. Our platoon broke into four lines and we were doing some exercises around camp. We arrived at the pull-up bars. This was the most challenging part of the official physical fitness test for me. Though I was small and fairly strong, I had gained about twenty-five pounds since high school. In order to score a perfect rating on pull-ups, we were required to do twenty. My personal max was only seventeen.

Somehow, Steve and I were next to each other in line as we arrived at the pull-up bars. We were always joking around when we didn't think we would get caught (or at least he was) and as Steve left the pull-up bar, he said something funny that caught me by surprise. As I went to pull up my first time, I burst out laughing. Guess who heard me? Yep, Sergeant Abolins was there again.

"Get over here Congultun!" Sergeant Abolins said. He had finally gotten my name right, or close to it anyway.

"Aye, aye, sir," I responded and then quickly made my way over to him trying to hide my smirk quickly.

"Something funny?!" he yelled. His mouth was duck-faced, his nose scrunched up and his eyes peered through me.

"No, sir!" I answered.

"Get over to that sand pit!" he yelled, "Go, go, go!" I immediately ran over to a sandbox area. As I arrived, he yelled again, "Get back here! Go, go go!" I ran back toward him. "Get back to that sand pit!" I ran back. "Get back here!" I turned around and ran back toward him. "Get away from me!" he yelled again and pointed to the sand pit. I ran back. I had started to work up a serious sweat in that southern California sun. "Now get down in that sand pit and give me twenty!" I dropped into push-up form and started pushing as fast I could. I was beginning to wear down, but I had to push them out. "Now, do fifteen snow angels face down and blow into the sand!" I almost laughed inside and would have if I had not been thoroughly exhausted at that point. "Now push! Fifteen more!" he yelled. "Now ten more sand angels!"

He got me worked up as quickly as possible and had me doing snow angels in the sand face down while blowing out, filling my face with sand. I was covered head to toe in sand which stuck to the sweat all over my body. Since we were in PT (athletic) gear instead of full camouflage uniform, I was drenched in sweat and sand. Much later, during our free time, Steve and I laughed over that experience and it was just one more opportunity that Sergeant Abolins had to convince us of how hard core he was.

Overall, boot camp was a living hell for me. *Physically*, I was able to handle it. *Emotionally*, I was spent. Thankfully Steve was there with me to try and "enjoy" it together, but I was miserable. I felt like I had gained three more people in my life just like my dad and I never knew when or how I was going to set them off. I hated life, but I knew I couldn't quit. I had to keep going. I just didn't know how. To top it off, my least favorite part was coming at my least favorite time. We were headed out into the field to camp for a week just as the weather was beginning to turn cold in November. I didn't know how I was going to be able to handle a week of training out in the cold field.

Chapter 24

Camp Pendleton (1992)

"AAAAHHHH!!! Help! Help!" I screamed. I wrestled about and toiled in my sleeping bag which completely enveloped my body. I had never slept in a mummy bag before and had no idea how to get out. I woke from a deep sleep and was trying to figure out where I was. I was trapped inside and couldn't escape as I was clamoring for air! I felt claustrophobic and began panicking! "Help, I can't get out!" I screamed again. I began to tear at my bag and literally began ripping my zipper from my bag as I toiled about.

I had also begun to turn my body around and sit up on my knees. This was a problem since our pup tents were only built for two Marines side by side and were about forty some inches high in the center. They formed a low ceiling A-shape and as I sat up on my knees, I pressed into the top of the tent. I continued to clamor for air and I was still trying to figure out where and when I was. *I had enough! I had to get out!* I stood straight up, continued screaming, and literally ripped my way out of my sleeping bag, tearing the zipper all the way down. My tent rose with me and lifted off the ground as I stood up.

It was dark and in the wee hours of the morning, but many of my fellow recruits that were sleeping nearby in our tent formation began to wake up. I finally broke free from the captivity of my sleeping arrangements and breathed loudly, gasping for air. As I looked around, I recognized that I was still in boot camp and we were camping out in the field. Several of my fellow recruits were trying to figure out what was going on with me, but when they realized that I was just freaking out due to being claustrophobic, they told me to shut up and go to sleep. They weren't too happy that I was intruding on what little sleep they were getting that night.

It was a brisk morning and as soon as I came to and realized what was going on, I also realized how cold it was. It was probably only forty degrees or so, but I started freezing and wished that I had not just torn things apart. I took a short walk, ten or fifteen feet back and forth to collect myself for a moment, but quickly gathered things back together. My tent buddy helped me reassemble and I laid back down in my sleeping bag. I think my neighbor was just a bit stunned as to what happened, but surely wanted to return to sleep quickly, as well.

As I laid back down, I tried to zip my bag up because I was feeling cold rather quickly. That's when I realized that I had torn the zipper from the bag. It no longer zipped up, but at least it had a few snaps that allowed it to stay semi-closed. After I snapped the few snaps, I turned it upside down to try and keep as much heat in as I could. I continued to wake up on and off the rest of the night shifting between claustrophobia and freezing from the cool air.

When I woke the next morning and for the next few days, I received the cold shoulder from my fellow recruits that slept near me. I could tell they weren't happy about being woken up.

On Sunday, we had chapel services in the field. We sat in metal bleachers that were there for training exercises. Every week during boot camp, I attended chapel services for two primary reasons. First, it was our only time and way to get away from the drill instructors. We had about an hour and a half of freedom. Second, I still loved singing songs. Many of the songs were more traditional hymns rather than the popular choruses that I learned at High Street, but I enjoyed them just the same. Steve had actually become our platoon lay-leader (non-professional spiritual leader) and led prayers each night before bed. I hadn't really paid this much attention yet, since it wasn't real personal for me.

That Sunday morning though, we sat in the bleachers and listened to a Navy Chaplain tell us about the lifestyle of many Marines after boot camp. He talked about how they go out to bars, get drunk and start carousing around. He talked about how they slept around. He talked about how sometimes Marines live such a party life that it will land them in big trouble with the Marine Corps itself.

I began thinking about my life and how I was a pretty good kid. My dad lived that drinking life he talked about, but I rejected it not wanting to turn out like him. I never drank an ounce of alcohol in my life. My dad was violent, but I refused to be that way. I refused violence even when I had the chance to hurt my dad back. My dad was racist. I refused that attitude and embraced equality. I opened myself up to learning about different types of cultures and their ways of living. My dad thought men were better than women and thought that it was okay to dominate them. I refused that mindset and knew that men and women are equal, just with different qualities and characteristics. My dad had been so selfish in life and abusive to us in many ways that I had been determined to never be like that when I had kids. I **never settled** for the example that he gave me.

Despite all of the ways that I felt I was not a bad kid, I knew I wasn't perfect and I needed a savior. I can't fully explain why. It wasn't a mental thing. It wasn't an emotional thing. It was a deep down thing. I believed the message that Jesus gave his life for me, I put my faith in Him, repented of my sins, and asked Him into my life. That morning, I stepped down out of the bleachers and went forward to pray. I told the Navy Chaplain what I thought and felt God was doing in my life and he led me in a prayer where I accepted Jesus into my life.

"Father, thank you for sending Jesus to die on a cross for my sins. Thank you for loving me when I cared nothing about you. Thank you for sending people into my life to share your message with me. I am sorry for the way I've lived my life. I have been selfish. I have sinned against you. I ask now that you would forgive me of my sins and wash me clean. I turn from my sin to live my life your way. I put my faith and trust in you, Jesus. Thank you for bringing me into your family and giving me new life! Amen," I prayed.

When I opened my eyes, I was filled with peace and joy that I had never experienced before. For the next week, every time I got a chance to read my Bible, I read it. When I read it, my heart got warm and I knew God was with me and speaking to me. Many of the other recruits in our platoon got angry with me for waking them up and I felt their disgruntledness. However, it didn't bother me. I was filled with the love of God and I was on cloud nine.

I figured out pretty quickly that God wanted me to change the way I spoke. In my prayer when I asked Jesus into my life, I repented of my sins. To repent means to turn the other way. I had to change the way I lived my life. I grew up around people cussing all around me. While my dad never *let* me cuss, he never filtered his language around me. As a small guy, I used to joke that I had little man's disease which meant that I ran my mouth a lot and cussing was definitely a part of that. I knew that I needed to change the words I used. The Navy Chaplain didn't tell me that. Steve didn't tell me that. My Bible didn't even come out and say that in any particular way. I knew it deep down. God didn't want that type of unwholesome talk coming out of my mouth. It didn't reflect Christ well.

In the next week or two, I worked on not cussing. Habits can be hard to break, particularly bad habits. At first, I tried the drill instructor method. When I thought of a cuss word, I would say a replacement word such as friggin, dang, or shoot. Soon, I began to think of the replacement word instead of the cuss word. Then when I thought of the replacement word, I tried not to say anything at all. Pretty soon, I was able to not cuss at all any more. But it wasn't just about breaking a habit. I think anyone can do that with hard work and practice. My mind was changing. My spirit was changing. I was filled with peace and joy and the junk that filled my mind and heart before were gone. That was as big of a change as anything else.

When people spoke badly about me, I smiled. Instead of hating them for it, I loved them. I was being changed from the inside out. God had given me a new spirit and a new attitude. I smiled a lot more. I was happy. The first two phases of boot camp were incredibly hard, particularly emotionally. But now I was filled with new energy and motivation to keep going! I felt like a new person. I stopped talking crap to people I didn't like and I started to keep any negative opinions to myself. My world was being changed upside down.

A week later, we moved out of the field and back to San Diego for the third phase of our training. When we got back to the recruit depot, we noticed the other recruits that were still in the first phase of their training and we could see an incredible difference! They were slobs. They didn't know how to march. They didn't hold their heads high. Their cadence was off beat. What we quickly realized was how far we had come and that we were nearly through! We were almost Marines!

Our first week back in San Diego, we were given a week of service. During this week, we didn't do any of our normal training, each recruit performed a particular service that he was assigned. Steve and I volunteered to help clean the General's office building because we heard that chow hall duty was the worst and we didn't want that.

At first, we were afraid to go into the General's building. If we were to say something wrong, look less than respectful or forget to salute someone, we would be court martialed and kicked out of the Marine Corps before we even got started. Or at least, that's what we were afraid would happen. But we quickly found out that this was a cake job. Our job consisted of cleaning an already super clean building and polishing the brass everyday. We typically did our cleaning after everyone left the building after their normal work day. Steve and I had the building to ourselves.

We found a room that had a phone with long distance service. We would look out for each other and then call home to talk to our girlfriends and/or family. Crazily, we snuck these phone calls that we knew could get us in pretty major trouble if we got caught, but it was only for a week and the risk seemed worth it. We missed home desperately and were ready to be done. Thankfully, we never got caught.

Once our normal training resumed after our service week, Steve and I had another great idea. We chose firewatch duty every other night. Firewatch was a security duty where two recruits would walk around the barracks for an hour keeping a watchful eye for any problems. Steve and I volunteered for the same hour about 3 a.m. every morning so that one of us could sneak phone calls on the payphone in the stairwell. Steve called Heidi just as she was waking for school and I called the girl I was dating before we left. We knew the same risks awaited us during this time, but we took it anyway. And we never got caught. The week before graduation, I received a letter from my girl. She told me she decided to move on and started dating someone else. I was saddened, but I wasn't heartbroken. I knew God was with me and that was all the encouragement I needed.

I continued to attend chapel services every week and was filled with God's presence. I continued to read my Bible and soaked everything up. I was learning everything anew since it was now very personal to me. I learned so much and God continued to bless me with His peace and joy. I even began to share my faith with other recruits from time to time when the opportunity allowed. Not all of them liked it, but that didn't bother me. I just wanted them to know the love of God. I prayed that they would.

The last three weeks flew by and before we knew it, graduation arrived. Heidi's family, Steve's mom and his sister all came to graduation. My parents didn't, but I expected that. I was just so thrilled to be done. That day was special.

We put on our dress blues with our white gloves and covers. We were sharp and we knew it. That morning, we marched together toward graduation with a pride that none of us had ever experienced before. We were Marines and we felt the pride.

"From the Halls of Montezuma
To the shores of Tripoli;
We fight our country's battles
On the lands as on the sea;
First to fight for right and freedom
And to keep our honor clean;
We are proud to claim the title
Of United States Marine"

We sang at the end of the ceremony. We stood proudly on Shepherd Field Parade Deck, proclaiming our allegiance to the

United States Marine Corps and the United States of America. We were ready to take on the world.

That was the most significant thirteen weeks of my life. While I felt I had grown up when we lived in Northglenn and definitely Byers, I hadn't really grown up until I accepted Christ *and* became a Marine. Jesus changed my life on that eighth week of boot camp and I had earned the title, Marine. I walked with my head up, full of pride, joy and peace. That was, until God made me aware of one significant attitude in my life that needed to change.

Chapter 25

Forgiveness (1992 - 1994)

As I started to grow as a Christ follower, I became increasingly aware of what an amazing God I was coming to know. While God did help me to deal with both my present challenges of boot camp, he did much more to help me deal with my long term challenges from growing up the way I did. I had grown to hate my dad with a passion.

I was tired of losing people in my life. I longed for lasting relationships. I longed for people to be positive and wanted to have nurturing relationships where we would build each other up. I longed for someone to notice the good things I did in my life and choose to support me in them. I wished my dad had provided good guidance and a positive role model in my life.

Even though Mom was always loving and selfless, she wasn't able to protect us from my dad.

My dad had caused me to lose so many things. I lost my sister, Terri for most of her high school career. I lost my brother, Jimmy during his high school years. I lost several years of opportunity at the one sport I excelled at; wrestling. I lost most every friend I ever had until Steve. I lost any hope of having a loving, caring father. I lost having a mom who would protect me. I lost my innocence in so many ways at such a young age. I lost every chance I had of knowing a good, loving God.

But God interrupted all of that.

> "Whoever claims to love God
> yet hates a brother or sister is a liar.
> For whoever does not love their brother and sister,
> whom they have seen,
> cannot love God,
> whom they have not seen."
> 1 John 4:20

God changed my life in boot camp and my faith in Him grew immensely. I began to realize that I could not say that I love God and still hate my father. That made me no better than him. None of us are perfect, I was reminded. But I still knew that I could not keep hating my dad.

But I did. *He deserved my hate and anger*, I told myself. *How could God expect me to just let him off the hook? How fair was that?* I began to question God's logic. I wondered how He gave up His own son out of love for me. I wondered how God forgave me for everything I ever did. It took some time for me to get the idea that He truly forgave me of my past. Yet, I still wondered how He continued to forgive me when I continued to mess up even after I gave Him my life. I was even stuck with, *how could He forgive me for hating my dad?*

These questions took me on a journey where I learned more about God's love and forgiveness. God sent his son Jesus to die for me when I cared nothing about Him and was far away from a relationship with Him. I stood before God as His enemy, yet he forgave me. When I sinned against Him, I realized that it was as if I was nailing Jesus to the cross. *My* sin caused Him to need to be crucified. I was just as guilty as anyone that has ever lived. Yet, God gave Jesus to me anyway. He provided a way out. He provided a way to be restored, to be made whole. When Jesus died on the cross for me, He offered Himself as a sacrifice that would take my place. My sin condemned me to eternal separation from God, yet Jesus on the cross provided me the opportunity to be forgiven and experience eternal life with Him.

God forgave me. All I had to do was ask. All I had to do was repent. All I had to do was to put my faith in Jesus. God forgave me. *How could God do that? How could I do that for my dad?* When I thought about my own forgiveness, I learned what forgiveness meant. This provided me the very real possibility that I could actually, possibly forgive my dad.

For one, I learned that forgiveness was not saying that it was okay for him to treat me that way, that it wasn't a big deal. When God forgave me, He didn't accept my sin. He didn't say, "No problem, just keep on sinning and enjoy. It's no big deal." No, He never accepted my sin. Therefore, I didn't have to accept my dad's treatment of me. I didn't have to say, *it was no big deal.* I didn't have to say, *it was okay.* It was still wrong and it hurt me deeply. That was still very true.

Forgiveness did not mean there were no natural consequences either. Just because I needed to forgive my dad, there were still some very real consequences. Even though our family has found a way to live and laugh years later, we show many marks of the traumas we experienced. We are broken in so many ways. I am broken in so many ways and God continues to piece me back together and make me whole. Forty seven years later, I still struggle with emotional issues as a result of the way I grew up.

One small, silly example is that I still have an internal desire to constantly move. I fight against this desire so that my wife and daughters can maintain a stable home life. But this desire to move is so strong. I have two ways to help me deal with it. I rearrange my house and/or repaint a room every six months or so, so that I get a sense of change. We also take road trips quite often for vacation. My wife grew up in one city her entire life, but has now traveled to forty-nine states. Next summer we will hit number fifty together when we travel to Vermont. We get around on vacation. It helps me to deal with this constant desire to move. These natural consequences didn't go away just because I needed to forgive my dad.

I also learned that forgiveness was not pretending I wasn't hurt. Sometimes when my family gets together, we still laugh about all of the crazy times we had together. We laugh about all that we've been through and this is one of the ways that we've learned to cope with our messed up lives. But forgiveness is not pretending that it was all fun and games. It is not pretending that it wasn't extremely hurtful and we didn't lose a lot. When God forgave me, He also reminded me that Jesus went through a lot when He became human, to live life as we experience it and to go to the cross. I was reminded that He was beaten and a crown of thorns were placed on His head. I was reminded that He was literally hanging to his death on the cross, naked and bearing my sin upon Him. There was no pretending that my sin didn't cost God. He endured much pain for me. In the same way, I endured much, though mostly emotional pain by my dad's behavior and there was no pretending it away.

I learned that forgiveness was not a *feeling*. I was often confused because I did not feel like forgiving my dad. I learned that *I did not have to feel it.* I simply needed to do it. Sometimes, a positive feeling would follow. Other times, I would be reminded of the hurt and pain that continued to run through my memory and emotions. If I had waited for a feeling to come, forgiveness never would have happened. Similarly, God didn't wait until He felt like forgiving me of my sins. In fact, He sent Jesus long before I was even born. I learned that **God's love** is not a *feeling*. The Bible uses a particular greek word for God's type of love. It is called "agape" love, which means the *unconditional* love of God. God loves us without any conditions. That takes emotions out of the picture. Forgiveness is not about a *feeling*, it is about a *choice*.

I also learned that forgiveness did not mean I had to allow my dad to hurt me again. It is important to have boundaries and maintain expectations that I will be treated with dignity and respect. I did not have to allow my dad to demean me, talk bad about me or even continue to spend time with him if he didn't treat me well. Forgiveness was not giving him permission to hurt me again. He didn't have a right to do that. I would not allow it. God does not allow it in our lives with Him either. While we still are left with freedom of choice, God never okays our sin nor says it's no big deal for us to treat Him that way. He told me to repent of my sins, which meant; to turn away from them. He forgave me, but He didn't say it was okay to keep sinning against Him. God **never settled** for sin. I didn't need to settle for it either.

I learned that forgiveness was when I no longer held his sin against him. As I understood it, He was still on God's hook even though I let him off mine. I know that my dad deserved eternal separation from God for the way he treated me and my family. It was up to *God* to deal with him. I also know that *I* deserved eternal separation from God for the way *I* lived **my** life. God will deal with me too. I only have hope in this reality because I have an advocate in my life. His name is Jesus. When God deals with my sin, He sees Jesus and His sacrifice and lets me off His hook. I knew He would do the same for my dad, as well, if he put his faith and trust in Jesus. I no longer had to hold my dad accountable. My dad was accountable to God, not me.

After a few years of learning about these truths, God helped me to finally forgive my father. He helped me learn how to love my dad in spite of the way he treated me. He taught me that I didn't have to accept that treatment from my dad, but I did have to forgive him for it. God gave me a love for my dad that was unconditional. I learned to love him no matter what. I learned to care for him and to give grace to him, particularly in times that were difficult even many years later. I could have turned my back on my dad and never spoke to him again. I wanted that for a while. I could have held onto my anger and bitterness because he deserved it. But I **never settled** for what *he* deserved. I found life in love and forgiveness.

I read a great quote recently that said, "Grace is when somebody hurts you and you try to understand their situation instead of trying to hurt them back." I used to consider some kind of retribution toward my father. I thought, *maybe I could drive him to Indiana where he is wanted by the law and turn him in. Maybe I could beat him up,* I thought when I was younger. *Maybe I could destroy his record and CD collection, then he would get a sense of how badly he hurt me.* But I gave up all of these ideas when I forgave him. I gave up any possible retribution and decided to let God handle it however He felt best. And then I started praying for God to change his heart and give him the faith he needed to put his trust in Jesus. I continued to pray that daily. I **never settled** for him to simply pay the price he deserved.

I had an experience with my dad one day when I was about forty. The experience was deeply painful and reminded me of all the ways that my dad hurt me over my life. Emotional pain was still there and it was deep. However, I didn't hate my dad for it, nor did I seek retribution. Instead, God gave me the ability to try to comprehend what led him to do such a thing. God gave me the ability to consider, truly consider what type of pain and hurt that my dad must have gone through to treat his own son that way. My heart was crushed as I considered how broken my dad must be inside from his own life experiences.

Over the years, God has taken me on a journey and shown me things I never saw as a teenager. I hated my dad and all that he was about. I could not see any good in him. Yet, my dad gave me several things that have been a great benefit in my life. I believe the grace of God and His work in my life have now allowed me to see these things that I never saw before. God *never settled* for me to only see the bad in my dad, but He opened my eyes to some very positive things in him, as well.

Even though my dad was a bad role model, he demonstrated what *not* to be. While Dad was not religious in any way, shape or form, I sometimes wonder if that was a good thing. I wonder, if my dad had been overly religious (and yet, still harsh), if I would have rebelled against that and hated God for it. While I wouldn't have wished for it, I think Dad's lack of religion or belief in God actually helped me to stay open to Him.

Dad's drinking and associated behaviors with abuse have cemented in me a conviction to never drink alcohol. I don't think drinking in and of itself is wrong or bad or sinful, I just choose not to drink. I have a strong feeling that if I ever did, I would have ended up much like my dad. I am thankful that I have never had to struggle with that because I learned my lesson by watching him.

The way I saw it, Dad was selfish in the way he led his family. He was selfish in his moves, trying to leave his problems behind without considering the problems he was handing us. He was selfish in how he treated my mom when he was both physically and verbally abusive. He was selfish in how he disciplined us. It was rarely about our own good, but more about him releasing his anger. Dad taught me through my experiences how **not to** treat my wife and kids. *My* family, *my* wife and kids, have lived in one county in only four homes in the twenty-three years since my oldest daughter was born. I **never settled** to follow his example, I chose to live my life differently.

Dad did have some redeemable behaviors though, that did have a positive affect on my life. Dad was an affectionate father. He always loved to give us hugs and kisses. He was particularly fond of me and cuddled me a lot when I was young. Until my brother, Jimmy ran away, I was the favored one and it showed how often I sat on his lap and cuddled when we watched movies or TV. Even when he had been drinking, he would call me out to the car and have heart-to-heart talks with me. While I thought it was probably the booze doing the talking, it nevertheless opened my dad up with an honesty and authenticity he might not have expressed otherwise. While Dad did do damage from time to time physically, he was also very physically affectionate towards me.

Dad was also a compassionate man for people in need. We experienced a lot of hardships ourselves, obviously due to the life we lived. We often needed to ask for help and we often received it. So, whenever my dad saw someone else down on life and he had the ability to help them, he helped them. He was always offering someone down on their luck some assistance. He offered rides, food, music tapes, and even allowed some folks to live with us for a time. Dad was always compassionate to those in need if he had the means to do something about it.

Dad knew how to talk to people. He could talk to the wall for an hour if no one was around and have a great conversation! While I characterized this ability as manipulative and it often was, it was a gift. Dad was a great talker and could converse about just about any subject. He was not limited to a few of his favorite subjects; although, he did always find a way to weave music into the conversation. He was a genius when it came to his knowledge of music.

I have grown to appreciate his love for music and love it myself, as well. It was my own love for music that helped me enjoy church when I first started attending. My love for music still continues to this day and can be very therapeutic at times.

I think the greatest life lesson that I received from my dad was responsibility. In many ways, this entire story was me learning responsibility. When Terri and Jimmy left home to live in foster homes during their high school days, I went from being the youngest in the family who could do no wrong, to being the oldest who could do no right. I did not transition well and did not accept the added responsibility that was placed on me. Whether I agreed with my dad's parenting strategies or not, I now realize he was trying to teach me responsibility and I ran from it. Thankfully, it finally began to penetrate my life though.

It was this sense of responsibility that helped me play on athletic teams throughout junior high and high school. It was this sense of responsibility that helped me maintain a job while playing three sports each year in high school. It was this sense of responsibility that really hit home in Marine Corps boot camp and helped me become a man, helped me become a Marine. It was this sense of responsibility that helped me take responsibility for my own sin and trust Jesus to forgive me. It was this sense of responsibility that helped me to not just receive Jesus, but also learn how to forgive and love my dad. It was this sense of responsibility that taught me to *never settle*.

God gave me a new perspective on my dad and his place in my life. God gave me the ability to forgive. God gave me a new relationship with my dad. God gave me an unconditional love that is only possible by Him. Thanks to God, I can now say, **I loved that man.**

Epilogue

Life with Jesus, living His way and in His strength isn't perfect or easy. But it's so worth it. My dad and I have had some challenges over the last twenty plus years in our relationship. But I couldn't have done it at all if not for my heavenly Father who teaches me daily about unconditional love and forgiveness. No matter how challenging anyone's childhood was or wasn't, unconditional love and forgiveness is so very necessary. Living them daily can be just as challenging as experiencing them in a once-and-for-all kind of way.

As I mentioned earlier, my dad loved to talk. I do too, but I love to talk in person. My dad loved to talk no matter how it happened. Since we lived almost a thousand miles apart, we didn't see each other often enough. My dad would love for me to call him at least once a week. I would love to never have to talk on the phone. I just don't like to do it. My dad didn't believe that a parent needs to call their children. He believed it is their responsibility to call their parents to demonstrate love to them. I believe it should be somewhere around fifty-fifty and each should be calling equally. We disagreed.

His feelings got hurt. My feelings got hurt. I had to learn to see things from his perspective and consider how he felt. Yet, I also had to set boundaries for our relationship that were healthy. Sometimes when he was angry, he lashed out and called me names and degraded me. I still have much emotional pain in my body from my childhood that may never leave me regardless of forgiveness. This is another example of a natural consequence that I referred to in the last chapter. This pain creates emotional turmoil for me and I needed to step away from the relationship to recover and to set boundaries for the type of relationship I was willing to have. Sometimes, I needed to do that. I had to forgive again and learn to love again.

I am also learning what it means to be "in Christ" and a part of God's family as different and extended from my biological family. Though I was born and raised by my parents in a particular place in history, I am also now an eternal part of God's family. The implications to this reality are incredible and life changing.

When I was growing up watching sitcoms, I imagined what it would have been like to live with the Keatons on *Family Ties* or the Seavers on *Growing Pains*. I came home to a rough life in my own trailer in Byers and wondered why I didn't have their life. I decided for myself that I would pursue their kind of life. I would **never settle** for the life that I was given. It's incredible to think about today because I now live that kind of life with my own family (my wife and girls).

Our life now is more like an episode of Growing Pains. We experience all of the challenges that life throws at us with two working parents and two teenage girls (my oldest is now twenty-four and married). We have hardship at times, but we find ways to laugh about it and enjoy what we have. We get angry and upset, but we forgive and love and move forward. We listen to each other and do our best to meet each other's needs. We live in a stable home, have stable jobs and treat each other well. We have a lot of fun just hanging out at home or riding bikes together or taking walks. My girls amaze me all of the time for their maturity and excellence academically too. It is amazing what God can provide and give when you put your trust in Jesus.

My relationship with my wife is simply incredible. In some ways, I could write a whole book just on that. In other ways,

I'm left without words. She is an amazing woman and she loves me deeply. She supports me in many of the ways that I always wished I had been supported. We enjoy so many things together and we work through the difficult times and challenging emotions that come from living with and loving each other for twenty-six years. We always learn how to forgive each other and encourage each other through life's challenges. We love to spend time together traveling, walking, biking, and finding new places to eat together.

My family is so fun and enjoyable, but we are far from perfect. Each of us sins. We fall short, but we find forgiveness in Christ. We worship Him weekly and we spend time encouraging each other in small groups such as Young Life (for the girls) and our close friends from church. I meet weekly with a prayer partner who prays for me when I struggle and a group of guys that read the Bible and talk about how to live it out. We also serve in our community, both through our jobs and other opportunities. It is incredible what God can and does do when you put your trust in Him.

I hope my story, though sad and true will help you find your own hope. I hope you will learn to forgive those that have hurt you. Even if you do not believe in God, I hope you will keep an open mind and heart for those that do. I hope you will, at least, consider Him. God has changed my life from challenging beginnings to incredible ways today. Trust Him and He can change your life too.

Biographical Timeline

1. Camp Pendleton, CA
2. Fallbrook, CA
3. Camp Pendleton, CA
4. Griffith, IN
5. Hobart Twp, IN
6. Castle Rock, CO
7. Fair Oaks, IN
8. Paris, IL
9. Chrisman, IL
10. Horace, IL
11. Leiters Ford, IN
12. Rhinelander, WI
13. Lavina, MT
14. Jacksonville, FL
15. Black Oak, IN
16. Medora, IN
17. Roundup, MT
18. Bennett, CO
19. Morocco, IN
20. Portage, IN
21. Elizabeth, CO
22. Elbert, CO
23. Savannah, GA
24. Glenrock, WY
25. Grant Park, IL
26. Donovan, IL
27. Tefft, IN
28. Demotte, IN
29. Crandon, WI
30. Laona, WI

31. Monico, WI
32. Ingles, KS
33. Cheyenne, OK
34. Grover, CO
35. Reno, NV
36. Lovelock, NV
37. Tucson, AZ
38. Grover, CO
39. Ault, CO
40. Loving, NM
41. Loogootee, IN
42. Crawfordsville, IN
43. Portage, IN
44. Carterville, MO
45. Avilla, MO
46. Loogootee, IN
47. Sterling, CO
48. Crook, CO
49. Stratton, CO
50. Limon, CO
51. Taylor, TX
52. Huntingbird, IN
53. Hawthorn, NV
54. Missoula, MT
55. Washington, IN
56. Loogootee, IN
57. Seymour, IN
58. Taylor, TX
59. Pine Bluffs, WY
60. Cloverdale, IN
61. Sheridan, IN
62. McCook, NE
63. Windfall, IN
64. Hudson, CO
65. Bailey, CO
66. Grant, CO

67. Deer Trail, CO
68. Agate, CO
69. Waterman, IL
70. Ransom, IL
71. Streator, IL
72. Agate, CO
73. Thornton, CO
74. Byers, CO
75. Byers, CO
76. Greeley, CO
77. Byers, CO
78. Deer Trail, CO
79. Loogootee, IN
80. Chicago, IL
81. Deer Trail, CO
82. Springfield, OH
83. Granger, TX
84. Byers, CO
85. MCRD San Diego, CA
86. Camp Pendleton, CA
87. MCRD San Diego, CA
88. Camp Pendleton, CA
89. Del Mar, Camp Pendleton, CA
90. Camp Johnson, Camp Lejeune, NC
91. Camp Johnson, Camp Lejeune, NC
92. Jacksonville, NC
93. Camp Lejeune, NC
94. Med Float in the Mediterranean Sea
95. Springfield, OH
96. Springfield, OH
97. Springfield, OH
98. South Charleston, OH
99. Springfield, OH

1 Peter 1:23 TLB

For you have a new life.
It was not passed on to you from your parents,
for the life they gave you will fade away.
This new one will last forever,
for it comes from Christ,
God's ever-living Message to (people).

Acknowledgements

None of this book would have happened if not for Jesus. He made a way where there seemed to be no way. He gave light to the darkness. He gave hope to the hopeless. He gave life where there was death. He is hope, eternal.

I need to thank my wife, first and foremost. She has loved me through the hard times. She has forgiven me for falling short too many times. She has helped me see another way to live life that I wasn't given in childhood. She has demonstrated Jesus to me, in the flesh. She has been my encourager, my number one supporter. She has spent many hours waiting for me to finish writing, editing and some other part of the book so that we can go do something together. She spent countless hours reading my manuscript and wondering how I came out of all of that. She told me how great it was, even if it maybe wasn't yet. She helped me see things that I missed when I was writing.

Next, I need to thank my daughter, Jordan who was my first editor, proofreader, and beta reader. Having just taken college English and being such a smarty pants helped so much! But more than that she was also an incredible encourager! For a girl who doesn't read for enjoyment, she told me how much she enjoyed reading my story and constantly praised me for both writing it and living it.

I have several friends who also served as beta readers, each providing their own level of editing, proofreading and personal feedback. I can't thank them enough. Thank you Terry Sowers, Stephanie Burley-Jones, Chris LeMaster, Jeremy Hudson, Todd

Buck, Michael Manley, Michelle Carn and Tanya Anderson. Each of them poured over my manuscript and gave their best feedback and more importantly, encouraged me throughout the process. Thank you to Amya Boyer (Twitter: @amyaproofreads), a new proofreader in the business who offered to proofread my manuscript for free!

I thank my family, starting with my mother who read and reread the story. I can only imagine how painful it was to relive parts of the story. I thank her for always loving me and showing me what Christ looked like in the midst of our turmoil. Thanks for correcting all of the details that a little boy didn't remember. :) Thanks to Terri, who read the entire thing in a day. Thanks to Jim (Jimmy) who provided some correction on details and a small portion of his own story in chapter 12. Thanks to Shelby for providing her little sister versions of some of the stories. Thanks to Shannon, Jesse, and Jason for putting up with my poor leadership and lack of responsibility as a teenager. It has been so strange to hear how your childhood was so different than mine since we were siblings. It's crazy to think how much you grew up *after* I left home for the Marine Corps.

I thank my mother-in-law, Rosemary Kellis for loving me into the Kingdom. For showing me and telling me about Jesus. For treating me like a son, long before I became her son-in-law. For encouraging me in every way as a follower of Christ and as a person. I hope she is encouraged by her prominence in my story. Oh yeah, thanks for your daughter too, Rosemary, I love her.

Shawn D. Congleton has lived a life on the move; moving nearly 80 times before he graduated and living in almost 20 states. Since that time, he has spent most of it in Ohio with his wife, Heidi and three girls, Morgan, Jordan, and Brooklyn. He has been an admin clerk for the United States Marine Corps, secretary for Wright State University, youth and young adult pastor at High Street Church of the Nazarene, church planter with Life House Community, secretary with Springfield-Clark Career Technology Center, school counselor for Dunbar High School and Springfield High School, and co-principal with his wife, Heidi at the Eagle & Dove Academy.

CPSIA information can be obtained
at www.ICGtesting.com
Printed in the USA
BVHW031646090223
658228BV00012B/68/J